S 1 D

HUMAN RIGHTS FOR
THE 1990s

HUMAN RIGHTS
FOR THE 1990s

LEGAL, POLITICAL AND ETHICAL ISSUES

Edited by
ROBERT BLACKBURN
and
JOHN TAYLOR

MANSELL

LONDON AND NEW YORK

First published 1991 by
Mansell Publishing Limited
A Cassell Imprint

Villiers House
41/47 Strand
London WC2N 5JE
England

125 East 23rd Street
Suite 300
New York, NY 10010
USA

British Library Cataloguing in Publication Data

Human rights for the 1990s: legal, political and ethical issues.
1. Human rights
I. Blackburn, Robert   II. Taylor, John
323

ISBN 0-7201-2035-7

Library of Congress Cataloging-in-Publication Data

Human rights for the 1990s: legal, political, and ethical issues/
edited by Robert Blackburn and John Taylor.
    p.   cm.
  Includes index.
  ISBN 0-7201-2035-7
  1. Human rights. 2. Human rights — Europe.
  I. Blackburn, Robert, Ph. D.   II. Taylor, John, C.M.G.
III. Title: Human rights for the nineties.
K3240.4.H834   1991
323 — dc20   90-39486
                                                   CIP

Printed in Great Britain by
Biddles Ltd, Guildford and King's Lynn

This book is dedicated
to the memory of
PAUL SIEGHART
and
LORD ELWYN-JONES

Contents

The contributors

Dr Robert Blackburn is Lecturer in Law and Director of the Centre of British Constitutional Law and History at King's College London. He is a Fellow of the British Institute of Human Rights.

Rt Hon Lord Elwyn-Jones was Lord High Chancellor of Great Britain between 1974 and 1979.

Professor Lawrence Freedman is Head of the Department of War Studies at King's College London.

Rt Rev Richard Harries is Bishop of Oxford and was formerly Dean of King's College London. He is a Governor of the British Institute of Human Rights.

Professor Rosalyn Higgins, QC, is United Kingdom Member of the United Nations Committee on Human Rights and Professor of International Law at the London School of Economics. She is a Governor of the British Institute of Human Rights.

Professor Ian Kennedy is Head of the School of Law and Director of the Centre of Medical Law and Ethics at King's College London.

Walter Merricks is Assistant Secretary-General of the Law Society of England and Wales.

Professor Paul O'Higgins is Professor of Law at King's College London and a Fellow of Christ's College Cambridge. He is a Governor of the British Institute of Human Rights.

Dr Richard Plender, QC, is Reader in Law and Director of the Centre of European Law at King's College London.

Professor Henry Schermers is a Member of the European Commission on Human Rights and Professor of Law in the University of Leiden.

Paul Sieghart was Chairman of the Executive of Committee of Justice (British Section of the International Commission of Jurists) and a Visiting Professor of Law at King's College London. He was a Governor of the British Institute of Human Rights.

John Taylor, CMG, is Director of the British Institute of Human Rights.

Introduction

This book contains a collection of lectures and papers delivered to the British Institute of Human Rights at King's College London between January 1987 and April 1990. The subject matter dealt with contains a rich variety of issues drawn from different parts of the vast spectrum which makes up the human rights field. It is hoped that the book will be of value at two levels: first, each individual paper constitutes an independent analysis of some topical or key issue by a leading writer or practitioner in the particular subject covered; secondly, the collection of papers taken together comprises an introduction to the study of human rights by serving to illustrate the wide range and diverse nature of what it is that human rights is all about. Care has been taken throughout to avoid the use of technical jargon and to present the text of each paper in a manner palatable to all categories of human rights readers, whether undergraduate, professional or interested layperson, whether philosopher, social worker or lawyer.

It was in early 1986 that the British Institute of Human Rights moved its offices to the School of Law at King's College London, and so began the present successful collaboration between these two bodies, both of which for many years had been at the forefront of the movement in the United Kingdom to promote a greater awareness and understanding of human rights principles. The British Institute was founded in 1970 with the following aims: to establish itself as a reference centre; to promote education in human rights and participate in academic discussions; and to launch and assist in related research projects. Among its many activities in the two decades since its foundation have been the gathering of a large collection of published literature on human rights, giving evidence to a House of Lords Select Committee on a Bill of Rights in 1977, the production of a report on Freedom of Religion in Western Europe for the British Council of Churches, and collaborating with the Policy Studies Institute on a project to clarify the role of international human rights law in British industrial relations. Many of the contributors to this book have served on the governing board of the British Institute, including Rt Rev Richard Harries, Paul Sieghart, Professor Rosalyn Higgins and Professor Paul O'Higgins.

At precisely the same time as the British Institute was being brought into existence, the School of Law at King's College London was pioneering the study of human rights at University level. In 1970 and 1971 Sir Francis Vallat, Professor of International Law at King's, put together a remarkable series of lectures on human rights affairs to be delivered by a distinguished range of speakers which included Lord Denning, Lord Caradon, Professor René Cassin and Professor James Fawcett. Early in 1971 the Senate of London University approved Sir Francis Vallet's draft syllabus for a postgraduate LL.M. course on human rights. This was launched in the 1971–72 session and continues to the present day. During that time and since, scholarship and research at King's College in the human rights field have progressively gathered momentum, frequently providing a focus for its more specialised bodies such as the Centre of European Law, and extending also into departments other than law, especially philosophy, history of political thought and international relations.

The study of human rights is the study of the whole of human nature. Most of the contributions to this book are concerned with law and it is to legal methods of protection for citizens, both within states and across them, that much of the post-1945 international concern for human rights has been addressed. However, the relationship and balance between the competing rights of man and society contain many lines of inquiry prerequisite to any true understanding of human rights law, or what it is that the law is seeking to achieve. 'Human rights' as an expression may have a modern ring to it, but as a science it is as ancient as Plato and Aristotle, and no more genuine interdisciplinary subject exists than the study of human rights. The very suitable first chapter to this book, 'Human rights in theological perspective', is provided by Richard Harries, Bishop of Oxford. The paper was delivered as a lecture when he was Dean of King's College London. Another important contribution to the book is 'War and human rights' in Chapter 2, where Lawrence Freedman, Professor of War Studies at King's, writes of human rights in the context of armed international conflict, occasions which in our modern history have proved the most subversive of even the most basic rights and freedoms of individual human beings as well as to racial and social minorities, and which in the case of World War II led directly to the United Nations Declaration of Human Rights in 1948 and to the European Convention on Human Rights and Fundamental Freedoms in 1950.

Among the contributions by lawyers there is a deliberate mixture of style and approach. In Chapter 4 Lord Elwyn-Jones, who is now greatly missed following his death in December 1989, reflects upon the relationship between 'Judicial independence and human rights' from his experiences in the late 1940s as a prosecutor of Nazi war criminals, to his thoughts in office as Lord Chancellor between 1974 and 1979 on the necessary qualities of a judge in the British legal system. Similarly, experiences and reflections by persons holding important offices are given by Professor Rosalyn Higgins on 'The United Nations Human Rights Committee' on which she sits; by Professor Henry Schermers of the European Human Rights Commission on 'The right to a fair trial under the European Convention on Human Rights'; and by Walter Merricks of The Law Society on 'Human rights and legal services'. Traditional scholarly analyses are given by Ian Kennedy, Professor of Medical Law and Ethics at King's College London, on delicate and complex ethical issues in 'Patients, doctors and human rights'; by Dr Richard Plender, QC, Director of the Centre of European Law at King's, who, in the chapter 'The legal protection of refugees', expounds on the role of law in dealing with the frequent international crises concerning the movement of refugees; and by Professor Paul O'Higgins on the important but neglected subject of the benefits and problems posed by 'The European Social Charter'. In 'Legal and political arguments for a United Kingdom Bill of Rights', Dr Robert Blackburn presents some of the rationale behind the proposal for adopting the European Convention on Human Rights into the domestic law of the United Kingdom. Finally, Chapter 3, 'International human rights law: some current problems' by Paul Sieghart is a classic review of the state of international human rights law by one of the most forceful human rights campaigners of his generation. Sadly, Paul Sieghart died only a short while after delivering the completed text of his paper. It is to his memory, and that of Lord Elwyn-Jones, that this volume is dedicated.

It is important for readers of this collection to note that the written texts of these papers were completed at different times. The texts of Chapters 1, 2, 4, 5 and 8 were completed in 1987; Chapters 3, 6 and 7 in 1988; Chapters 10 and 11 in 1989; and Chapter 9 in 1990.

The editors are indebted to the authors in this volume for their generous support in terms of their time and their helpful co-operation in publication.

It is very much hoped that publication of this collection of papers will help stimulate further interest and inquiry into the vital and multi-faceted subject of human rights theory and practice.

March 1990   R.B.
                                                                                    J.T.

Human rights in theological perspective

RICHARD HARRIES

Human dignity

The concept of human rights is usually assumed to be a secular notion; and the emergence of human rights in the philosophies of the late seventeenth century, culminating in the French Revolution in the late eighteenth century, a secular movement. This needs qualifying. The American Declaration of Independence in 1776 declared: 'All men are created equal, (and) are endowed *by their creator*, with certain unalienable rights'. Indeed, as we know, the founding fathers of the United States and of the constitution were devoutly, fiercely Christian. We note too that the French made their declaration in 1789 'in the presence and under the auspices of the Supreme Being'. No less important is the fact that the truths inherent in and safeguarded by the concept of human rights were, before the eighteenth century, expressed in other ways and guarded by other means: the accountability of sovereigns to God; the divine law; and the position of the Church, at least before the Reformation, as a countervailing power to the unbridled tyranny of the state.

From a consciously Christian point of view rights are grounded, first of all, in the value of the created order. I say rights, rather than human rights at this stage, because it may be that others besides humans, animals for example, have rights. One of the features of our time is the movement to conserve species of animals and plants and to preserve the environment from pollution. There are millions of birds in the world and hundreds of species. Why should some men and women devote a great deal of time and trouble, say, to preserving a species of wild guinea-fowl in the tropical forests of South America? They recognise and value the richness and variety of creation; the inherent worth of every form of life.

So the question of rights is wider than human rights. Nevertheless, it is on human rights that we now focus. All talk about human rights presupposes a recognition of the dignity and worth of the human person. On the whole moral philosophers are shy of saying anything as basic as that. But Christian theologians are not, or ought not to be, ashamed of being counted with the babes and sucklings out of whose mouths unadorned simplicities can

This chapter was submitted in 1987.

come. And even moral philosophers will on occasion admit to what, of course, they believe. So Ronald Dworkin writes:

> Anyone who professes to take rights seriously . . . must accept, at the minimum . . . the vague but powerful idea of human dignity.[1]

'This idea is associated with Kant', continues Dworkin. One wonders why Kant is singled out rather than the framers of the legal codes in the Old Testament, or Jesus, or Aquinas, to suggest just a few of the thousands of pre-Kantian alternatives. For the worth and dignity of the human person is basic to the Judaeo–Christian–Islamic tradition. This could be illustrated by countless writers from all three religions and talked about in a variety of ways. I will focus on some fundamental Christian doctrines as a way of highlighting the point. First, human beings are created by God; and, moreover, created in his likeness. We are not the chance by-product of a random and ultimately meaningless splurge of life on a small cooling star. We are the deliberate creation of an eternal and loving spiritual reality. He who is the source of all value has chosen, as it were, to break bits off himself. But that metaphor, though deliberately chosen, is wrong. For when God broke bits off himself he brought into existence creatures with a real independence. As the old Jewish metaphor puts it, God picked up the skirts of his clothing to create a tiny space where he was not, in order that there might be a space where free creatures could live. All creatures, because they come from God, share in something of his value. But human beings, who are able to choose, think, pray, and love, are said, because of these special qualities, to have been created in his image.

Here a protest must be entered against one assumption that lurks around in the religious unconscious. It is that the creator can do what he likes with his creatures: that they have no rights against God. I am sorry to say that this view is found even in Paul. Using a picture derived from Jeremiah that God is the potter and human beings his pots, Paul argues that we have no right to complain if some are selected for salvation and others are not.

> Man, who art thou that repliest against God? Shall the thing formed say to him that formed it, why hast thou made me thus? Hath not the potter power over the clay, of the same lump to make one vessel with honour, and another with dishonour?[2]

But even staying with this analogy, the conclusion is not what Paul would have us believe. For the potter has not just tossed off the pot. He has worked at it for day after day, indeed for aeon after aeon. He has literally sweated blood over it. He has, literally, put his heart and his soul into it. The pot that is produced, flawed though it may still be, is infinitely precious to the creator. Or we can put it another way. God creates and at once recognises the value of what he has created. Here is the foundation for a consciously

Christian approach to human rights: *God makes man in his own image and respects the worth and dignity of what he has created*. With this affirmation both Jew and Muslim would agree. But the Christian wants to go even further. Such is the value of human persons in the eye of their maker that he himself becomes a human person; he takes to himself human nature that they might share his divine nature. The Good Shepherd goes out for the one sheep that is lost, hunts high and low for it until he brings it home to eternal life, rejoicing. Human beings are that precious in the eyes of God.

The violation of human dignity

In a family governed by harmony there would be no need for either parents or children to talk about rights. The value of each person would be fully recognised and respected. The language of human rights is necessary because in the world as a whole that is not the case. Human beings are tortured, imprisoned without trial, discriminated against, kept in permanent poverty and so on. It is necessary to assert rights in order to protect human persons from this cruel and degrading treatment. In short *the basis of human rights is not simply human dignity as such but the fact that this human dignity is so often denied in practice*. This second aspect is likewise fundamental to the Christian view, which has always insisted that human life as we know it is fatally flawed. As Reinhold Niebuhr put it:

> Though Christ is the true norm of every man, every man is also in some sense a crucifier of Christ.[3]

It is from this two-sided truth that the Christian Church seeks to construct a Christian policy. It is because of this that it has both affirmed the state as an expression of the essentially social nature of human persons and argued for the tragic necessity of a coercive power in the state, without which human social life would not be possible.

The state, in Christian theology, is in principle a divinely sanctioned institution. But states are ruled by sinful human beings. As sinful human beings need the power of the state to curb their lawlessness, no less do the rulers of the state need a curb on their potential for oppressing their citizens. From this follows all the classical checks and balances of liberal democracies, the separation of powers, elected governments for a fixed term and so on. These classical democratic arrangements are an expression of a belief in the freedom and dignity of citizens: but no less, and perhaps more importantly, they express the fear of tyranny that is incipient in every human government. It follows then that from one point of view human rights legislation belongs to the emergence and refining of the democratic tradition. For human rights express the dignity of human beings, and also seek to protect that dignity against arbitrary powers of government.

Utilitarianism

A theological perspective on human rights will therefore respond positively to Dworkin's distinction, in his discussion of utilitarianism, between personal and external preferences, a distinction he believes that has not been properly taken into account in other discussions on human rights. Utilitarianism is based on preferences. But these preferences may be personal, for example a white student may prefer segregation because it improves his chances of getting into law school. Or his choice may be external, that is, he dislikes black people and disapproves of social situations when the races mix. The problem, according to Dworkin, is that in practice – that is in a democratic society which is based on the preferences of its citizens – it is not possible to differentiate between personal and external preference. There is therefore the likelihood of inequality being built into the system. For the system will inevitably reflect not just what citizens want for themselves but their attitudes to others. For this and other reasons Dworkin champions what he calls a strong sense of right.

The concept of an individual political right . . . is a response to the philosophical defects of a utilitarianism that counts external preferences and the practical impossibility of a utilitarianism that does not. It allows us to enjoy the institutions of political democracy which enforce overall an unrefined utilitarianism, and yet protect the fundamental right of citizens to equal concern and respect by prohibiting decisions that seem, antecedently, likely to have been reached by virtue of the external components of the preferences democracy reveals.[4]

Utilitarianism is the underlying assumption of liberal democracy, but all societies depend on some collective goal or idea. Human rights, in Dworkin's view, are a safeguard for the individual against any such idea of the common good. In his famous phrase they are political trumps.

Individual rights are political trumps held by individuals. Individuals have rights when, for some reason, a collective good is not a sufficient justification for denying them what they wish, as individuals to have or do, or not a sufficient justification for imposing some loss or injury upon them.[5]

If someone has a right to something, then it is wrong for the government to deny it to him even though it would be in the general interest to do so.[6]

To take a contemporary example, in a society of limited resources there might be a widespread distaste of homosexuality in general and those with AIDS in particular. A democratic government, responsive to the popular mood, might deny those with AIDS adequate medical care. It could mount an argument that this was in the common interest, in the sense that it reflected the preference of the majority of the citizens. Or, in an undemocratic country, the government might just decide that it was in the common interest that AIDS victims should die untreated, as a deterrent to others. In either society there needs to be a right to equal medical care; a right that belongs to every citizen whatever a government might or might not decide was in the common interest.

In a perfect society human beings would be able to make personal preferences, and at the same time both sympathise with and respect the personal preferences of others. But we lack that imaginative sympathy and respect. Even if we have it in some degree we are inclined to let our personal preferences ride roughshod over other claims. In short, the distinction that Dworkin makes, and which is inherent in the democratic societies we know, corresponds to the twin insights of Christian theology: our capacity for love and our denial of love; our ability to recognise human dignity in theory while denying it in practice.

Human rights are *natural* rights. By that is first of all meant the fact that these rights can be recognised by all people, whatever their religion or lack of it, whatever their politics or their ideology. Hitherto I have discussed the consciously Christian basis of human rights, about human beings being made in the image of God and yet crucifying that image of God. Yet it is equally part of Catholic tradition that human beings have value, and that this value can be recognised as such, without any conscious religious belief. There is, according to Catholic tradition, a natural law and, corresponding to this there are natural rights. ˙

Natural law and natural rights

Natural law has been subjected to attacks from three quarters. First, there have been those Protestant thinkers who, emphasising the corruption of the human race, have denied the capacity of natural, unredeemed man to respond to moral law. This is manifestly absurd, and in fact has the effect of undermining the Christian faith. For how can Christians come to recognise Jesus to be 'the way, the truth and the life', without some inkling of what is the way, the truth and the life. Secondly, there are legal positivists who deny the existence of any laws or rights that are not already present in legal form. But a Theistic view of the world will always want to insist that human laws ultimately derive their validity from, and are subject to correction by, a higher moral law. The moral obligation to obey the law is not derived from the law itself, and law is, rightly, in a constant process of flux. Unjust laws, such as the Group Areas Act in South Africa, are not morally binding (though it may be deemed prudent on occasions to adhere to them). Thirdly, moral philosophers have sometimes doubted whether the concept of natural law has any meaning. Certainly few today would want to defend the thesis that what occurs naturally, that is, in unimpeded nature, is *ipso facto*, a design carrying moral obligation. However, what is protected by the concept of natural law is the conviction that human beings are moral beings; that irrespective of any religious beliefs they have the capacity to recognise moral truths; and that whatever differences of culture or religion may divide us it is possible for people of differing backgrounds to engage in moral discourse with one another on the basis of at least some common assumptions. Indeed the development of modern human rights law is a remarkable tribute to natural law in this sense. From the United Nations Charter in 1945 to the latest Instrument of the ILO people of the most diverse backgrounds have agreed on a long series of laws and rights. This agreement and the discussion that produced it presupposes capacity for moral, and not just legal, discourse that belongs to human beings as such: that is *natural*.

Some, in the natural law tradition, see natural law and natural rights as being closely bound up. Jacques Maritain, for example, after arguing that human beings, as such, have a destiny and that destiny is natural and therefore obligatory for us, wrote:

> If man is morally bound to the things which are necessary to the fulfilment of his destiny, obviously, then he has the right to fulfil his destiny; and if he has the right to fulfil his destiny he has the right to the things necessary for this purpose.[7]

Whatever reservations moral philosophers may have about natural law there appears to be less reluctance to use the phrase *natural* rights. There are, of course, still those who say, like Bentham, that it is a nonsensical notion and that talk of them as 'natural and inprescriptible' (that is, inalienable) is just 'nonsense upon stilts'. But, from a Christian perspective, they exist; not just as legal rights but as moral rights which undergird and subject to improvement all legal rights. These rights are *natural*; that is, they belong to all human beings *qua* human beings and they can be recognised as such by everyone whatever their religious convictions.

Christian suspicions of rights

Although, as was suggested earlier, Christians were active in the formulation of rights in the American Declaration of Independence, and though the concept of natural law contains an implicit recognition of human rights, there is nevertheless a niggling doubt in some quarters about whether talk about rights is really compatible with Christianity. This doubt must be examined. First, there is the idea that a creator can do as he likes with his creatures. Creatures, it is said, have no rights: and this, if true, seems to undermine any idea that creatures have rights even between themselves at the creaturely level. But, as we argued earlier, God has created man in his own image: and *God himself recognises and respects the supreme worth of what he has created.*

Secondly, there is the notion that Christian ethics is an ethic of duty, rather than rights. Even if this is true, duties presuppose rights. My duty not to murder presupposes the right of other human beings to life. But it is not certain that the Christian faith is committed to a duty-based, rather than a goal-based, right-based, or value-based moral philosophy. It is true that the common starting point for Christian action is doing the will of our heavenly Father. But this will is for the well-being and flourishing of his creatures. How we decide what will make for their well-being and flourishing is illuminated by the biblical revelation. But in moral reflection on this, the notions of right, good and value, as well as duty, all have a place. Indeed, if Christianity is committed to the idea of the worth of each individual person (as opposed to any collective goal) it would seem to favour the move being made in some quarters towards a right-based moral philosophy.

Thirdly, there is the idea, derived in particular from the Sermon on the Mount, that Christians should be in the business of waiving their rights rather than asserting them. This raises very complex and disputed questions of how we are to interpret and apply the perfectionist strand in Christian ethics. My own position is that this element, focused on the Sermon on the Mount, acts as an absolute standard which judges all our human compromises, but that it does not, under the conditions of sinful finite existence, take away our civic duties and rights. We have both duties to the state and rights under it. Luther was quite wrong to tell those taking part in the Peasants' Revolt of 1529 – 'Suffering! Suffering! Cross! Cross! This and nothing else is the Christian law.'[8] As he emphasised our duties to the state, so he should have urged, no less strongly, our rights under it. Those rights exist whether or not individual Christians choose in certain circumstances to waive particular rights. For, of course, there is the world of difference between choosing to waive one's own rights – the right to sue, for example, as mentioned in Matthew 5:40 – and urging others to waive theirs. Rather, in the world in which we live, a world in which there are so many powerless, Christian love is best shown by championing the rights of the weak, and expanding the areas in which their rights are respected, against the vested interests of the powerful.

Unfolding rights

Human rights are rooted in moral values. Because of this legal recognition of rights is a dynamic historical process. It is as the result of a gradual – too gradual – process that rights have become enshrined in declarations, conventions and covenants that go to make up International Human Rights Law.

First it was the barons who obtained recognition of their legal rights in the Magna Carta of 1215, and not only their own rights but the rights of all freemen. Then came the Charter of 1354 when Edward III introduced the important concept of 'due process of law'. In the eighteenth century the process was speeded up and the bourgeoisie obtained some of the political and economic liberties that we take for granted in the West today. In our own century we have seen those political and economic rights being claimed by the great mass of human beings.

The fact that the legal recognition of rights has been the result of a long, slow historical process need not lead us back into a legal positivism or make us think that the concept of a natural right has no meaning apart from its legal expression. Dworkin draws a distinction between a concept and a conception. For example, the American Constitution lays down the concepts of 'due process of law' and the equal protection of the law for all citizens, but it did not tie future citizens to the particular conceptions of due process and equal protection in force in the late eighteenth century. Yet guided by these fundamental concepts they were to express conceptions of them in varying circumstances. As a father, who tells his children to act fairly, does not tie them to his own notions of fairness, but urges them to work out differing conceptions for different circumstances, so we might say, that there is a natural right of every human being to equal respect and concern; but the unfolding of the implications of this is the result of a long series of political and legal decisions. A natural human right is, in Kantian terminology, the combination of a transcendent ideal with a categorical imperative: a combination about which some philosophers are sceptical but one which Christian theologians, for whom both fact and value are ultimately grounded in the being of God, are sympathetic to.

Nor does the idea of truth being revealed by a long historical process embarrass theologians (though some would reject the possibility). As the doctrinal truths of the Bible were only spelt out as the result of a process of development so also ethical truths have taken time to be seen in their fullness. In the early Christian Church there was a new equality before God. Rich and poor, bonded and free – all shared the common meal and knew they were equally subject to the just judgment of a loving God. As Paul wrote:

> There is neither Jew nor Greek, there is neither bond nor free, there is
> neither male nor female: for ye are all one in Christ Jesus.[9]

The full implication of that epoch-making text has not even now been fully secured legally, politically, economically, or even ecclesiastically. Yet the history of the West over the last 1,000 years can be seen, in part, as a grasping of its implications.

One of the disadvantages of the old natural law concept was that it blinded people to the dynamic, developmental possibilities inherent in ethical insight.

The ruling picture, taken from the political structures of the time, is hierarchical, submissive and static. The super-sovereign, God, gives his eternal law. Human beings through the use of their reason reflecting on nature, grasp this as natural law. In addition, God reveals his divine positive law. The two are brought together by secular rulers and the Church to provide laws, both secular and ecclesiastical, for Christendom. All is revealed, and all is enforced through a hierarchy from God to the lowest magistrate. The human duty is to listen, submit and obey. Some basic rights are, of course, preserved in this system. From time to time prophetic voices, like that of Francisco de Vitoria in the sixteenth century, pointed out ways in which basic rights were being denied. But this magisterial, architectonic system hardly encouraged the drawing out of insights that challenged and called for change in the received wisdom.

By contrast, modern theologians who are concerned with human rights associate them closely with Liberation Theology. As the phrase suggests, the central emphasis of this theology is that God is ceaselessly active in history, liberating human beings from all that enslaves and oppresses them. From the Exodus to the liberation struggles of today God is freeing people, not just from sin and death but from oppressive systems and structures. This involves Christians today in a new commitment to the poor, in line with God's bias to the poor revealed in the Bible. As Jose Bonino has put it:

For the vast majority of the population of the world today the basic 'human right' is 'the right to a human life'. The deeper meaning of the violation of formal human rights is the struggle to vindicate these larger masses who claim their right to the means of life . . . the drive towards universality in the quests of the American and French revolutions, the aspirations in the UN Declaration, finds its historical focus today for us in the struggle of the poor, the economically and socially oppressed, for their liberation.[10]

Again, Moltmann, who has written a number of essays on human rights, has said:

I think that only with this concrete starting point in the theology of liberation can universal theories and declarations about the freedom of man be protected from their misuse.[11]

The modern context

Since World War II the main sources for Christian reflection and comment on human matters have been not so much the works of individual theologians as the Vatican in the form of various papal encyclicals[12] and the World Council of Churches (WCC) through the pronouncements of the General Assemblies. I do not wish to comment on these in detail: suffice it to say that they have played their part in forming the general commitment to human rights that has produced the current body of human rights law. I want to look rather at a few of the major intellectual issues that have emerged, to see how these appear in a theological perspective.

The modern human rights movement began immediately after the end of World War II as part of the determination to build a better world, a world in which what had happened in Germany could never happen again. Some of the pressure for human rights has continued to grow from the desire to protect individuals from brutal governments, whether in South America, Africa, or the Middle East. But the human rights movement, not least in its Christian form, has also been shaped by two other major factors. First, Communism in the Soviet Union. For here is not just one more example of an oppressive government from whom the individual needs to be protected: here is an ideology which offers a particular challenge, both intellectual and practical, to the whole liberal notion of human rights. We may summarise that challenge under three heads. First, liberal notions appear, from a Marxist standpoint, too individualistic. Secondly, they are therefore too much concerned with individual freedoms and too little with the basic necessities of life; those necessities which are a basic right for all people and which must be a priority for governments to obtain them. Thirdly, from the liberal standpoint, the USSR has seemed gravely to violate certain fundamental freedoms.

The World Council of Churches, of which the Russian Orthodox Church is a member, has tried to maintain a delicate balance between affirming the fundamental freedoms that are dear to liberals, including Christian liberals, while not jeopardising the precarious position of the Orthodox, who are required to be loyal to policies of their government.

The other major factor, besides Soviet Communism, that has shaped the Christian debate on human rights is the concern, particularly by Roman Catholics in South America, for the basic necessities of life at present being denied millions of poor by oligarchies working in conjunction with world capitalism. From this is derived the close connection between human rights and liberation theology that has just been mentioned. From this point of view human rights as a championing of the individual against the power of the state has seemed very much a European concern. What is wanted, on this perspective, is intervention by the state on behalf of the poor against the tyranny of unrestrained capitalism.

Intervention for the most vulnerable

These different contexts and needs highlight the fact that human rights are not a static once-for-all achievement, but rather a moral imperative that requires constant appraisal and application. Nevertheless, these rather different emphases can be held together by Christian theology.

First there is the supreme value of each individual, as has already been discussed. But in Christian theology man is a social being. Mind itself is social reality. Man is made in the likeness of God not as a solitary individual but as a person in relationship, reflecting the relationship within the Trinitarian Godhead. The end of man is the communion of saints – a fellowship of persons knit together by love.

This has important implications for human rights. For it means that free-booting individualism is a denial of the essential nature of human person-hood. We are persons only in relation to other persons. The other person's welfare is my welfare. It means too that the state, which expresses and builds up man as a social being, has a particular responsibility for the well-being of all its citizens. The function of the state is not simply to mark out the pitch or mow the grass so that free individuals can compete with one another. The state has a duty to intervene to safeguard the interest of the more vulnerable, for they too are members of the whole and it is the welfare of all people as part of the whole that is at stake. If the Christian emphasis upon the dignity of each individual acts as a check on all views in which a collective goal is regarded as supreme (not least the Communist vision) the Christian emphasis on the social nature of man rules out a merely minimal concept of the state. This is reinforced by Christian insight into the sinfulness of man. For if the presence of sin necessitates checks and balances on the potential tyranny or rulers, it no less leads to the necessity of state intervention against the unrestrained pursuit of gain by the strong, and the need for a protective cloak around the most vulnerable.

This debate about the nature of political society is reflected among moral philosophers in the debate between freedom and equality. In the Western liberal tradition the freedom of the individual has long been regarded as the most fundamental of human rights. H. L. A. Hart has written:

> If there are any moral rights at all it follows that there is at least one natural
> right, the equal right of all men to be free.[13]

More recently Ronald Dworkin has argued that, on the contrary, the most fundamental of rights 'is a distinct concept of the right to equality, what I call the right to equal concern and respect'.[14] Dworkin argues that this is in fact the deep theory underlying our notions of fairness, including the well-known account of John Rawls.[15] Dworkin does not sit lightly to free-dom. On the contrary, he has argued that the just requirement of a system based on equal concern and respect is to take seriously the choices of each individual.[16] How better to treat them equally than to give them equal choice. Nevertheless, it is equality that is fundamental for Dworkin and his formula of equal concern and respect has distinct theological reverberations. It immediately calls to mind a God who, it is said, values every hair of our head; a God who mixes with the rejected and invites them into his Kingdom of Eternal Life. In Dworkin's view the concept of equality leads to the legitimacy of positive discrimination in favour of the deprived. Positive discrimination is also to be found in the Bible. The biblical God is a God of the poor, the rejected, the despised: and he intervenes on their behalf so that the last shall be first. In the person of Jesus, who is the poor person *par excellence*, who sums up the theme of outraged and innocent suffering that runs through the Bible, in Jesus the crucified, God intervenes on behalf of the powerless. Jesus is raised from the dead: the last is made first, and in him all those who are last will be first. The Bible is a book about positive discrimination. Its theme song is an imperative to discriminate in favour of the marginalised: and its triumph song is an affirmation of God's vindication of the powerless. It is the right of those whom Franz Fanon called 'The wretched of the earth' – to life, to the basic necessities of life, to the human dignity we all share – that is the most pressing of human rights problems in theological perspective today.

The idea that the state is founded on a contract is a fiction that some have found useful and it goes back earlier than the seventeenth and eighteenth centuries, when the idea came into prominence. But there is an older idea still, that of a covenant: a solemn, binding agreement between God and man. On his side God promises loving kindness and faithfulness. In return he asks of man – what? To share in his work; to share in the risk of creation. Creation is a risk: some of the time it seems a risk that was not justified. But God invites us to share in his great work, his work for the well-being and flourishing of all his children. In particular he invites us to share his commitment to the most vulnerable, to ensure their rights as human beings.

Notes and references

1. Ronald Dworkin (1984) *Taking Rights Seriously*, p. 198.
2. Romans 9:20–1.
3. Reinhold Niebuhr (1940) *Christianity and Power Politics*, p. 2.
4. Dworkin, *op. cit.*, p. 198.
5. *Ibid.*, p. xi.
6. *Ibid.*, p. 269.
7. Jacques Maritain (1944) *The Rights of Man and Natural Law*, p. 37.
8. Luther (1953) 'Against the robbing, murdering hordes of peasants', *Luther's Works*, Vol. 46.
9. Galatians 3:28.
10. Jose Miguez Bonino (1980) 'Religious commitment and human rights: a Christian perspective', in Alan Falconer (ed.), *Understanding Human Rights: An Inter-disciplinary and Integrated Study*, p. 32.
11. Jurgen Moltmann (1977) 'The original study paper: a theological basis of human rights and of the liberation of human beings', in *Allen and Miller* (eds), *A Christian Declaration on Human Rights*, p. 32.
12. Michael Walsh and Brian Davies (eds) (1984) *Proclaiming Justice and Peace: Documents from John XXIII to John Paul.*

13. H. L. A. Hart (1984) 'Are there any natural rights?', in Jeremy Waldron (ed.), *Theories of Rights*, p. 77.
14. Dworkin, *op. cit.*, p. 12.
15. *Ibid.*, p. 182.
16. Ronald Dworkin (1978) 'Liberalism', in Stuart Hampshire (ed.), *Public and Private Morality*.

2

War and human rights

LAWRENCE FREEDMAN

■

My objective in this chapter is to explore tension between the requirements
of National Security and a concern for human rights. I intend to challenge
the view that war and human rights are necessarily poles apart. Indeed I will
argue that, in surprising ways, war has often been good for human rights
and that in other, equally curious, ways human rights have been good for
military preparedness.

One has to start with some definition of human rights. I am going to take
a reasonably narrow but, I hope, acceptable focus on basic political rights:
freedom of speech, thought and association, with the addition of accountability
of political elites as an important right in itself. Saying what you want, with
whom you want, when you want is important, but it is also necessary to have
some access to the political system.

It is generally assumed that whatever the overall political system, military
systems themselves do not encourage human rights. The virtues of a military
system relate to discipline and loyalty with a hierarchy involving chains of
unaccountable command. Allowing privates to discuss the next tactical step
is not normally considered good military practice. The examples from the
Spanish Civil War of anarchists trying to fight on the basis of participatory
democracy are not desperately encouraging. Consequently any militarisation
of society is inevitably held to mean an attack in some way or other on civil
rights. It requires an extension of discipline and hierarchy.

None the less, this sort of militarisation of society can be justified as a
defence of civil rights in two particular ways. First, and this is a frequent
rationale for coups, a greater military role can serve as a means of introducing
discipline if the civilian society is breaking down into a form of anarchy.
It is argued that only by restoring a degree of order is it possible to create
conditions in which political rights can flourish once again. So military coups
often arrive with promises of an eventual return to democracy, even though
these are often honoured more in the breach than in the observance. Second,
the reduction of civil rights in the short term in war can be justified if this
is to protect them over the long term against an external threat.

This chapter was submitted in 1987.

When an external threat turns into war, governments find it necessary to extend control and reduce choice in more areas – labour, conscription, suspension of elections, censorship. Even a small war like the Falklands, while not leading to anything extreme, certainly led to some extension of political control. There were no formal measures introduced by the government, for example, with censorship of the media, yet there was a degree of moral pressure. Those who asked awkward questions could be said to be giving aid and comfort to the enemy or were putting the lives of 'our boys' at risk. Such pressure is very difficult to resist. (It is notable that many of those involved and subject to these strictures were retired military people adding to their pensions by commenting on the course of the war on the television.) During World War II formal restrictions were understood and accepted by the British people. By and large as a country we appear to tolerate our liberties being curtailed during war: our way of life is at stake and this requires restrictions on that way of life. Because information is an important military asset, if it flows too freely there is a risk of giving away too much to the enemy about one's plans and capabilities.

That is in war. In peace time it is much less tolerable, especially when the character of the external threat is controversial in itself. Throughout the past years of Conservative government in Britain there has been a persistent debate concerning the extent to which limits should be placed on free speech for the sake of national security. On the one side there is the argument that the abuse of liberties undermines national security. On the other side, the view is that a specious national security rationale is used to undermine liberties – with the *real* motive one of deflecting domestic political challenges to the state rather than external challenges from the Soviet Union. This set of issues has been raised consistently over the 1980s. One only has to mention the Belgrano, Zircon and Westland affairs, as well as the saga of Peter Wright's memoirs. The question of what is a legitimate secret and what is proper free speech has come to the fore of the political agenda.

Later, I will suggest some ground rules for handling this problem. Anybody working in the area of defence policy cannot but be aware of the rather grey dividing line between those matters which are and which are not secret. The distinction is by no means based on objective criteria. But before this, let us consider some of the more general propositions concerning the tension between national security and human rights.

▌▌

We can approach this through the nuclear issue simply because these weapons have been seen to give new twists to this particular argument. There is a common perception that in a nuclear crisis the speed of political decision would be such that fateful decisions – not only for the future of the country, but for civilisation – would have to be taken in a matter of minutes. The notion of the four-minute decisions is now ingrained in popular culture. Such a time-scale demands centralised decision making so that even in democratic systems no form of public pressure could be brought to bear. Annihilation without representation!

The content of the decision has also changed. In World War II we accepted a degree of risk and sacrifice because of the costs that we would have faced if the Nazis had been successful. The choice was between making a fight of it or accepting Nazi domination of Europe. Now the choice is said to be between accepting Communist domination, and the denial of human rights presumed to be entailed, or accepting the end of life itself; red or dead. This, it is argued, is a fundamental flaw at the heart of our national security policy, for it is no choice at all. When it is put like that, clearly, given the choice, most people would rather be red. At least then you have the option or possibility of the human will reasserting itself and changing the oppressive system which has been imposed. Without life there is nothing left and nothing to be done.

However, 'red or dead' is not the natural or inevitable choice. In Stalin's Russia or in Pol Pot's Kampuchea it was possible to be both red *and* dead. The assumption that the only threat involved is one to civil liberties, to a democratic way of life, perhaps distorts the nature of the choice. Furthermore, and more seriously, it is the function of strategy to avoid choices of this nature being forced upon us. And here strategy has succeeded: we have managed to avoid becoming either red or dead.

Can we trust those responsible for national strategy to maintain this success? What about the argument that the nature of nuclear decision making itself precludes democratic accountability and thus the exercise of our liberties? I believe this misstates the problem. It is true that ultimate nuclear decisions might be taken in a matter of minutes, but it is very unlikely that such decisions are going to suddenly arrive out of the blue, without a period of intense crisis in the international community and a degree of warning that such a decision might have to be faced. In fact the debate that has taken place within the Western democracies during the 1980s illuminated a lot of the issues that would face government in such crisis. It gave us, if not quite a dress rehearsal, at least some indication of the arguments that would readily come to the fore as soon as it became at all possible that NATO might have to implement its strategy of flexible response, and in particular that part that apparently requires us to threaten to initiate nuclear war.

From this experience we can suggest that one of the likely features of a crisis would be pressure upon government to reduce the risk of nuclear war. Toning down nuclear threats could become a very important part of domestic crisis management. Therefore it does not seem to be the case that nuclear decision making precludes accountability. The very prominence of nuclear weapons in our strategy ensures that the question of how they could be used is being addressed constantly and this process would probably intensify during the course of a political crisis. Already this questioning has led to the modification of the strategy and a reduced reliance on threats of mass destruction.

▌▌▌

At this point some might argue that this demonstrates the important inhibitions that would be placed on Western democracies in a crisis, which would not be suffered by their most likely enemies, the Soviet Union. In the Warsaw Pact there would be no effective public opinion. I am not sure that effective public opinion is wholly absent in these societies but it is undeniable that the channels of democratic accountability are weak compared with those of liberal democracies. Is it the case, therefore, that totalitarian societies have an advantage over liberal democracies when it comes to preparing for and fighting for war? The common view, certainly in the military, is that we accept a degree of inhibition as one of the costs of democracy. Liberal states cannot be prepared to fight wars as well as totalitarian states.

There is less in this than one might imagine. It may be the case that in times of peace democratic societies find it harder to direct resources towards defence when faced with the competing demands on public expenditure. It may also be the case that this contains its own dangers, in that government may be tempted to inflate the threat in order to generate sufficient support for those expenditures they do want to make. Theodore Lowi wrote a couple of decades ago an influential article entitled 'Making democracy safe for the world', in which he expressed concern over this tendency to exaggerate the dangers in the international system in order to justify domestic military expenditure and rather mundane overseas commitments. Command economies probably devote more resources to the military matters without having to provide exceptional and exaggerated rationales (though they often do).

But does this advantage hold in war? War is a testing time for any society. Most societies when they engage in total war, if not always in peripheral wars, have to rely on the whole-hearted support of the population. Governments that rely on repressive means to maintain control face two fundamental disabilities that at times of war can become quite chronic. First, maintaining a repressive society in itself imposes demands on the military system including a diversion of resources to police the state. Should the system grow in unpopularity, this diversion can become cumulative. To the extent that military forces are used for domestic repression they tend to be less suited for coping with the quite different strategic problems posed by confrontation with the conventional armed forces of another state. So the need to sustain a system of domestic repression in itself requires considerable expenditure of resources, and provides the wrong lessons for the military involved. It does not particularly make for efficient fighting forces.

Secondly, an understanding of the limits of popular support is critical to the waging of a modern war. This was after all what the Americans discovered in Vietnam. We did not go on quite long enough to discover it in the Falklands, but even then there were certain sensitivities all the way with regard to what public opinion would and would not bear.

It is one of the advantages of a democratic society that they have mechanisms that make it possible to gauge the degree of popular support for high-risk and high-sacrifice policies, and to see whether methods to increase popular support are or are not working. Totalitarian societies do not have this advantage. It is only necessary to consider the panic in Moscow in 1941 as German forces advanced, when they had no clear knowledge of whether the Communist Party had the support of their people and to what extent collaboration with the occupying German Army was likely. If the Nazis had been able to modify their own Nazism, and had been able to operate a much more sensitive policy towards the local population, they cold have been seen less as occupiers and more as liberators. As it was, Nazis could not stop being Nazis. (Occupying armies are often received initially as liberators, but they have a terrible habit of outstaying their welcome or not doing the right thing when they arrive.) The panic within the Soviet system in 1941 was partly surprise caused by the speed and efficiency of the German advance, and partly a fear of how their whole system could cope with the shock it was about to receive. Not for nothing were the war aims changed from the protection of socialism to that of the motherland in the great *patriotic* war.

I believe this is still a concern with the Soviet leadership in Eastern Europe. The performance of allies is a critical problem in the defence equation. The five divisions facing Czechoslovakia were put there not to face West Germany, but to face the Czechs. Now they also face West Germany, even though they are garrison forces for the Czechs. It is difficult to know whether these forces would be needed as a garrison or could be used against NATO. This is a major uncertainty for Warsaw Pact planners.

Without that essential information about popular feeling, totalitarian societies are often more brittle than democratic societies. War is therefore likely to be the breaking point for them. They are more likely to get into military adventures, and are equally more likely to be broken by them. This is why I was suggesting that war may be good for human rights. If you look at some of the major breakthroughs there have been in particular states with regard to human rights, these have often been the direct result of unsuccessful war. Why did Franco in Spain prefer not to get involved in World War II? Possibly because he was aware of the strain it would put on his system. West Germany and Italy are now accepted as wholly democratic societies in the modern system because of their post-war shift away from the extreme right.

Among the beneficiaries of the Falklands war were the Argentine people, because it ended the military junta and introduced the way for democracy. The Portuguese junta in the early 1970s collapsed because of the unpopularity of its colonial wars. The Greek colonels' regime collapsed because of its sponsorship of the coup in Cyprus.

Military adventures may offer hope for unpopular regimes, but if they fail they usually sound the death knell. The same is not true of liberal democratic society, because liberal democracies by their nature have a means by which it is possible to transfer power from the incompetent and the belligerent to the more pacific and – hopefully – more competent. Liberal democratic regimes are not always more successful in war – but they may find it easier to survive failure.

There are, of course, counter examples where war has been extremely bad for human rights. Certainly when war brings about the disintegration of society, whether it be Kampuchea or the Lebanon, the consequence can be disastrous. Wars – or war scares – can also leave an unfortunate legacy in liberal democracies such as the Official Secrets Act. None the less, to the extent that war tests societies, those who have developed a popular base are most likely to survive, and civil liberties are one means of developing such a base. A further twist to this is provided by an American academic called Michael Doyle. In a remarkable piece of research he demonstrated that liberal regimes do not fight each other. He looked at the development of liberal systems from 1800 and saw their steady growth, found them fighting illiberal regimes and colonial wars – but not each other. There are some grey areas, but by and large it seems to be the case that liberal regimes do not naturally go to war against similar regimes.

That again indicates that the advantages claimed for liberal democracy, as a reasonably efficient form of government and as one that guarantees human rights, ought not to be dismissed cynically. There is evidence to suggest that liberal regimes are less warlike (at least with each other). The democratic system allows the tests of war to be faced more effectively than it is by repressive regimes, even though it may well be the case that repressive systems are more likely to have developed the wherewithal to fight because of the advantages of a centralised command society.

IV

What then is the implication of this for policy? If it is accepted that human rights can strengthen a state in the international system, and that their promotion can be justified in terms of both international peace and national security, to what extent on the one hand should the universal promotion of human rights be an objective of foreign policy, and then, on the other, to what extent is it still necessary to accept restriction on our civil liberties, our political rights, in order to preserve national security? The answer is a matter of degree, and cannot be separated from questions relating to the broader issues at stake.

The most recent attempt to make human rights the centre-piece of foreign policy came with President Carter. His experiences revealed all the difficulties of this sort of approach. It is very difficult to establish good tests for another's political system. The democratic norms which we may accept in the West are not necessarily accepted elsewhere, and not necessarily authentic if imposed. The policy generated great uncertainty among many American allies in the Third World who felt they were being subjected to an artificial political test. In particular instances it proved very difficult to make human rights an overriding objective. You cannot suddenly ignore the Soviet Union or Iran or South Korea or Latin American states simply because they do not have your form of government. There are interests at stake with these states from supplies of raw materials to arms control agreements. Qualifications were necessary in the human rights policy out of respect for these other objectives, but that created a tendency for double standards to be introduced. It was possible to be absolutely beastly when it came to abuses of human rights by a weak state in the international system, but necessary to be more circumspect and temperate in language when it came to strong states. That in itself was not always an edifying spectacle.

States must examine closely their own records and behaviour before casting this sort of stone. There is a danger in being self-righteous when the evidence does not justify it. As the Soviet Union was challenged by Carter, it retaliated by discovering the rights of Red Indians, Catholics in Northern Ireland and the Basques in Spain.

One cannot even be sure that as a result of this pressure things will improve. There is no control over the countries themselves. Take for example Ethiopia. One of the reasons after the overthrow of Emperor Haile Selassie for the Americans' move away from the support of Ethiopia was the Dergue's appalling record on human rights. It is by no means evident that that United States was without means of transforming that unhappy country, but what is pretty clear is the American pressure was wholly counter-productive. In the end, Ethiopia simply ended up in the Soviet camp and the abuses continued.

International co-operation is also needed to pursue such a policy. If you refuse to sell arms to a particular country, because of its dreadful human rights record, it is not particularly helpful if a country with fewer scruples comes along and grabs the order.

The problems of making human rights the centre-piece of foreign policy are particularly evident when it comes to the nuclear issue. This can be posed not in terms of whether *we* wish to be red or dead but whether we wish to help others stop being red. In doing so, are we prepared to accept the risks of being dead? That is actually how the issue is likely to arise. The crisis may well be less one of Britain suddenly being subjected to a nuclear threat, but of a challenge to the position of Berlin or West Germany or a crisis in Czechoslovakia or Poland.

It may well be a case that without the fear of war, the West would have been tempted to do much more to help those that were struggling for their political rights in the East. Nuclear weapons make us more circumspect. We have had to say to those in the East that we can provide them with rhetorical and diplomatic support, but not military. They are on their own.

There are unavoidable limits to how far we can promote human rights in the Communist world. When trying to promote better relations with the Soviet Union some get irritated by those who are promoting human rights against what is seen as the greater benefit of international peace. Senator Jackson's fault was partly in the way that he did it, but others objected to the principle of linking trade measures to the release of Soviet Jews. In the end, his attempt – in 1974 – was so blatant that it backfired: fewer Soviet Jews were able to emigrate than would have otherwise been the case. Countries like the Soviet Union prefer not to be seen to be bending under pressure. Even Mr Gorbachov, defending *glasnost*, has taken great care to insist that liberalisation measures are not a result of direct pressure from the West. The Soviet Union asserts (oddly for a Communist state) the principle of non-interference in another's internal affairs.

When the consequence of confrontation is not so horrendous, then human rights do provide a rationale for going to war. It would have been far harder for the British government to develop national support for the Falklands campaign if the regime Britain was fighting had not been a military junta, as well as being white and right wing. If it had had a liberal democratic government then war would have been less likely for a number of reasons. Human rights provides one of the factors by which we judge other nations. It is a material factor and not just a propaganda line. In the Falklands, it was material in terms of what the occupation of the Falklands meant for the inhabitants – to be governed by a regime with such an unpleasant record.

Lastly, let me return to the question of the tension between national security and human rights at home. Secrecy is a question of political judgment. Few would argue that there are no genuine secrets. My starting point for judging what is a genuine secret is operational relevance. Details of a new radar system or code books, or how submarine sonars are going to operate are genuine secrets. So are details of a 'back-up' negotiating position at arms control talks. All these are legitimate secrets in so far as it is important that they remain so if the government and the military are to fulfil their responsibilities. At the other extreme, many of the assessments upon which government policies are based need not be secret. A proper debate on the wisdom of government policy requires the broad assessments upon which it is based being made public and intelligently discussed.

Sometimes these assessments are wrong, based on dubious information and questionable analysis. To take full advantage of the potential of liberal democracy with regard to the general lines of policy, requires information and analysis to be provided by the government so that is can then be challenged by its critics.

Unfortunately, in Britain governments start from the presumption that everything that passes through the government machine is a secret. Whether or not it is *really* a secret is not an issue. The onus is on others to drag it out of them. Information may be released as a result of clever questioning: it is less often volunteered. Only when governments find it important to support their own case in public debate does information suddenly find its way into the public domain. That is why the question of what is a secret is a matter of political judgment.

Let me take the familiar example of the question of Trident. From 1965 until 1980 there was not a single debate in the House of Commons on the subject of British nuclear weapon policy. Parliamentary questions over this period provide a quite remarkable *lack* of information and so their brevity is not surprising. There is in fact little published officially on nuclear weapons throughout the whole period in which Labour governments have been in office in this country, for there was also no debate on the matter from 1945 to 1951. The 1947 announcement that Britain was indeed producing atomic bombs was slipped in at the end of a parliamentary question and no encouragement was given to any editor who chose to draw attention to this development.

There was no serious public debate on whether Britain should be a nuclear power during this period, though there was a modest internal debate. The next Labour government in 1964 decided to carry on with the Polaris programme. The secrecy is not too hard to explain. Nuclear weapons pose very embarrassing problems for a Labour government. They would rather not talk about them. Debate was again discouraged in party political management.

The Chevaline Programme to improve Polaris was set in motion under the Tories, but was only really developed by the Labour Party in 1974. This was a programme that went over cost and was based on dubious assumptions about Britain's nuclear needs. It was kept wholly secret with only a few hints in the press. There was nothing in the annual defence estimates.

With the Conservative Party of the 1980s it has been different. The amount of information we have had on nuclear policy has been far greater than in the preceding years. A lot of it has been very interesting and the detail has been substantial. I do not believe that this is because of differing attitudes towards government information, but because this government was not embarrassed by this issue yet was under pressure to argue its case. Because it was necessary for the government to defend its position, it released relevant information that would not have been considered suitable for public eyes under other circumstances.

None the less, despite all the extra information, one still finds odd examples of things that are secret. For example, one secret is the date when the first Trident submarine will become operational. All the government will say is that this will be 'in the mid-1990s'. Are they going to launch it in secret? The reason why the in-service date is a secret is that it might slip. If you said the first boat was going to be available in 1994, and it did not appear until 1995 or 1996, something would have gone wrong. You do not want to set yourself up for a political scandal unnecessarily – so you keep it vague.

A further factor is industrial. A lot of classified material is not stamped 'restricted' or 'top secret' but 'commercial in confidence'. Awkward information might not affect British national security but could affect the position of major defence contractors – especially if one of their systems does not work very well. Release of information might harm export orders and therefore jobs. My argument is therefore that political reasons help explain why national security is invoked so often to justify secrecy. This does not mean that secrecy reflects a desire to stifle civil liberties. It is just because it is often more convenient to keep things quiet.

The conclusion I draw from all of this for those worried about national security being used to undermine civil rights in the United Kingdom is to exercise those civil rights. The more they are exercised, and the more intelligent questions are asked of government policy, the more likely it will be that the cover of national security cannot be used to hide important issues that deserve public debate. In this situation, genuine secrets that do deserve protection are less likely to be dragged up. When everything is secret, everything becomes fair game for investigative journalists. To keep secrets, you must be very clear about your criteria.

This has been the theme of this chapter: to challenge the view that national security and the promotion and enjoyment of political rights are often in tension. There are limits imposed upon each by the other. None the less, the advantages of a democratic society are still there in promoting intelligent debate, in developing popular support for policies, in criticising unwise policies and in being able to withstand most of the shocks that a modern society can face. Leaving aside whether any political system could survive the ultimate nuclear shock, there is every evidence to suggest that a liberal democratic system is as good and indeed better at coping with the shock of conventional war than a repressive system. In peacetime we should exercise our rights in all areas, including defence. In doing so we would not only have a more healthy democratic system – but also improved national security.

3

International human rights law: some current problems

PAUL SIEGHART

Human rights law is a subject that needs to be considered in the context in which it is embedded – politics, economics, and the lives of the innumerable people whom it can affect. Throughout the period in which I have had an interest in it, my prime concern has been to try to communicate its importance to those who are not its own scholars: first, *practising* lawyers; better still, those who are experts in other disciplines, like health professionals, scientists, politicians, and journalists; best of all, ordinary people who are not experts in anything, but for whose benefit the entire subject exists and who, through the exercise of their collective power as the holders of what we now call 'international public opinion', are uniquely qualified to promote its ever wider application – provided they know, at least in general terms, what it is about. What follows begins with a consideration of the origins of international human rights law, before turning to some problems with which it is presently confronted.

The origins of international human rights law

It is important to appreciate that it is only in very recent times that human rights has become part of the subject matter of international law, so that one may today properly speak of a positive and binding legal code of human rights law on the international plane, at a level well beyond the often vague and debatable claims in which all discourse about human rights necessarily had to proceed in the past.

One of the central concepts of international law has always been that of 'sovereignty', precisely because its main (if not for a long time its only) concern was with the relationships between sovereigns – orginally sovereign princes, and only later their successors, the sovereign nation states.

All legal systems operate by ascribing rights and duties to the various entities with which they deal, and correlating these symmetrically with each other; so that, whenever A has a right, there must be a B who has a corresponding duty. The primary right which international law ascribed to a prince (and

This chapter was submitted in 1988.

so, later, to a nation state) was his right of sovereignty, and the primary duty of each prince was therefore to respect the sovereignty of his fellow princes. Sovereignty, in this context, meant – and still means – the unfettered exercise of power within the prince's 'domain'; that is, the territory over which he ruled, and the individuals within that territory who owed him allegiance, originally called his 'subjects' but now more usually described as the state's 'citizens'.

Within his domain, the prince had the right to do as he pleased. In the context of his territory, this was called his 'territorial' sovereignty; in the context of his human subjects, it was called his 'personal' sovereignty. Any infringement of his sovereignty by another prince was, in international law, a wrong inflicted on him, which in turn gave him the right to seek various forms of redress. So, for instance, if one prince invaded the territory of another by armed force, that other would not only have the obvious right of armed self-defence, but also a right to undertake certain reprisals – such as impounding any of the other prince's assets which he found within his domain until the wrong had been righted, in order to obtain just compensation for it.

In that context, international law could, quite logically, have no concern for the rights and obligations of princes and their subjects towards each other. How a sovereign prince treated his own subjects, or later a nation state its own citizens, was entirely their own affair. Accordingly, the notions of 'civil rights' and 'civil liberties' which began to be developed in the domestic law of England in the seventeenth century and found their first full flowering almost simultaneously in the French *Déclaration des droits de l'homme et du citoyen* in 1789 and the US Bill of Rights in 1791, for a long time found no echo in international law. Private individuals could not be the subjects of that law: they were the subjects of their princes, having only those rights which they were allowed on the level of 'national' or 'domestic' law. There was just one exception to this: how a sovereign prince treated aliens – that is, the subjects of another sovereign prince – *was* a matter for international law, for any maltreatment of them might constitute an infringement of the personal sovereignty of their own prince, who might therefore be entitled to demand compensation – for himself, not for the maltreated subject.

A legal revolution

With only minor exceptions, this remained the position until as recently as 1945. However, by then it had become plain that this resolute shutting of international eyes to the state of affairs within a sovereign state held grave dangers for the international community of nations. The atrocities perpetrated on their own citizens by the regimes of Hitler and Stalin were not only moral outrages which 'shocked the conscience of all mankind'; they were a very real threat to international peace and stability. And so, there was carried through a veritable revolution in international law: within a single generation it developed a complete code of new law, enumerating and closely defining certain 'human rights' and 'fundamental freedoms' for all human beings, anywhere in the world, which were thenceforth no longer to lie in the gift of the sovereign states whose citizens these human beings were, but were said to 'inhere' in them 'inalienably', and so could not be abridged, denied, or forfeited – even by their sovereign rulers – for whatever cause. In the words of a great British international lawyer, Sir Hersch Lauterpacht, in 1950: 'The individual has acquired a status and a stature which have transformed him from an object of international compassion into a subject of international right'.[1]

The 'human rights' and 'fundamental freedoms' concerned were drawn from several sources: the classical 'civil and political' rights of non-intervention in the lives of private citizens, won in the revolutions of the eighteenth and early nineteenth centuries, such as the rights to life, to liberty and security, equality before the law, and fair trial, and the freedoms of conscience, belief, speech, assembly, association, and so on; and the 'economic' and 'social' rights developed in the later nineteenth and early twentieth centuries, calling upon the state to intervene in order to redress manifest and undeserved injustices suffered by individuals and the groups to which they belonged, such as the right to decent pay and conditions of work, to housing, health, education, and so on. (Although these latter rights owed much to socialist writers such as Proudhon and Marx, their implementation owed as least as much to writings which were not in the least inspired by socialism, such as Pope Leo XIII's encyclical *Rerum Novarum* of 1891).

These rights have been incorporated into international law partly through custom, but pre-eminently by the entry into force of a number of what are called 'law-making treaties', freely entered into by the sovereign states which constitutes the international community, and imposing binding legal obligations on them. What these treaties require is that the states concerned should 'respect', 'ensure', or 'secure' to every individual within their jurisdiction the rights which the treaties define,[2] 'without distinction of any kind such as race, colour, language, religion, political or other opinion, national or social origin, association with a national minority, property, birth or other status',[3] and that in the event of any violation of these rights the person concerned should have 'an effective remedy'.[4]

There is one more point which is central to any proper understanding of the modern code of human rights law: this code does not rank the rights and freedoms which it defines in any hierarchy, or any order of priority; nor is it possible to extract from it any consistent classification of them. One can group them, if one wishes, in a large number of different ways according to their various attributes, but all such groupings will be personal to the classifier, and therefore in some sense arbitrary. The treaties themselves treat all these rights and freedoms as having the same value – in a sense, the highest value that is possible in international law. Being 'inherent' and 'inalienable', they are paramount over all other rights and freedoms. Within the boundaries which the code itself defines for them – in order to avoid conflicts between them – no other kind of right or freedom can override them, deny them, or abridge them.

With that introduction, let me now turn to the problem areas which are the concern of this chapter.

Great expectations

The United Nations Charter was signed in 1945 in a spirit of abundant optimism. The forces of light had finally triumphed over the forces of darkness, symbolised by the Axis Powers; as at the end of the previous world war, there was a determination that such a cataclysm should never be allowed to happen again. But this time, the victorious Allies chose a different path from the one they had trodden in 1919: instead of imposing peace treaties on the vanquished, they sought to establish a new international *legal* order, founded on the three main principles declared in Article 1 of the UN Charter: the peaceful settlement of international disputes 'in conformity with the principles of justice and international law', and accordingly the outlawing of aggressive wars; friendly relations among nations 'based on respect for the principle of equal rights and self-determination of peoples'; and 'respect for human rights and for fundamental freedoms for all without distinction as to race, sex, language, or religion'.

However, by the time of the adoption of the UN Charter it had not proved possible to define in detail what these 'human rights and fundamental freedoms' were. In order to repair this omission, the United Nations proceeded to draft the famous Universal Declaration of Human Rights which they adopted three years later, on 10 December 1948.

Unfortunately, by then the United Nations had begun to become decidedly disunited and, although none of them opposed the Universal Declaration, eight abstained from voting: Byelorussia, Czechoslovakia, Poland, Saudi Arabia, South Africa, Ukraine, the USSR and Yugoslavia. Even so, it seems in retrospect nothing short of miraculous that such a detailed instrument should have been adopted *nemine contradicente* by 56 nations of such diverse political, cultural, and economic complexions, and one might be justified in wondering whether such a degree of consensus could be achieved today, were such a draft to come for the first time before the UN General Assembly.[5]

After that, further development of the new international legal order proceeded much more slowly. Conscious of the fact that the Universal Declaration was not a binding treaty in international law, the United Nations proceeded to try to transform its contents into detailed treaty law. But it was not until 1966 that they were able to adopt the product of much contentious drafting, in the form of the twin UN Covenants – the International Covenant on Civil and Political Rights (ICCPR), and the International Covenant on Economic, Social and Cultural Rights (ICESCR) – and it took yet another ten years before these two treaties entered into force in 1976.

During the same period, some of the world's different regions were elaborating human rights treaties of their own. The quickest exercise of that kind was undertaken in Europe, a region united by a common culture which had suffered most painfully from the human rights violations associated with the war; the European Convention for the Protection of Human Rights and Fundamental Freedoms (ECHR) was adopted as early as 1950, and entered into force only three years later, to be followed by a complementary European Social Charter (ESC), adopted in 1961 and entering into force in 1965. An American Convention on Human Rights was adopted in 1969 and entered into force in 1978, and the latest regional treaty, the African Charter on Human and Peoples' Rights, was adopted in 1981 and entered into force on 21 October 1986.

So the process of installing this new international legal order has taken a great deal of time, and most of it is still very young and therefore decidedly fragile. More than 40 years after the UN Charter can we say with any confidence that the international community of nations has accepted it?

Acceptance

If that community were governed by the same principle which it recommends for the internal governance of its own members – that is, majority rule – the answer would be yes. At the last count, 86 of the member states of the UN – that is, a bare majority – had ratified both the Covenants, and another four the ICESCR alone. All the 21 member states of the Council of Europe have ratified the ECHR, and 14 of them have ratified the ESC. Of the 31 members of the Organization of American States 19 – again, a majority – have ratified the American Convention on Human Rights; and 33 of the 51 members of the Organization of African Unity – another majority – have ratified the African Charter. There are even states, such as Switzerland and Liechtenstein, which are not members of the UN, but which are now bound by a regional human rights treaty.

However, there are still some striking gaps. Whereas the USSR has ratified both the Covenants, the USA has not: indeed, so far it has not ratified any human rights treaty, not even the Genocide Convention. Nor have South Africa, Saudi Arabia, and a number of smaller and less powerful states. In what sense then can they be said to have accepted the new international legal order which the founders of the United Nations were so determined to establish?

Here, we enter a realm of a complex academic debate. There is only one other candidate for an instrument representative of this new legal order, and that is the Universal Declaration. But it is clear from the text of this instrument itself that it was not intended as a treaty, let alone a law-making one. What then is its legal significance today? On this, scholars still disagree.

Some take the view that a Declaration which says, in its own preamble, that it is no more than 'a common standard of achievement for all peoples and all nations', who 'shall strive by teaching and education to promote respect for' the rights and freedoms which it declares, and shall 'by progressive measures, national and international . . . secure their universal and effective recognition and observance', cannot ever become part of binding international law.[6]

At the other end of the spectrum, scholars like Professor John P. Humphrey – who has the distinction, as the first Director of the UN's Division of Human Rights, of having prepared the first draft of the Universal Declaration – contend that, in the 39 years which have passed since its adoption, the Declaration has *de facto* become part of customary international law.[7] In support of this thesis, they point to the fact that, during this period, innumerable governments of the world's sovereign states – as well, of course, as the UN General Assembly – have cited the Declaration in support of some position they have adopted in international affairs (most frequently in criticising the human rights record of another state); that throughout this time not one such government has made any official pronouncement challenging the Declaration or any of its substantive contents; and that many of the new sovereign states which have come on to the international scene since 1948 have incorporated all or some of its contents into their national constitutions. These are powerful arguments, and they are supported by much evidence. So far, however, they do not appear to have convinced the two non-socialist states which abstained on 10 December 1948, namely South Africa and Saudi Arabia. (The others have now all ratified the Covenants.)

If Professor Humphrey's argument is right, then the Universal Declaration now binds all the world's sovereign states, including those few that are not members of the United Nations. But there are also other lines of argument which, if they are well founded, lead to the conclusion that the Declaration now constitutes a binding obligation at least for all the member states of the UN. The first of these is based on the Proclamation of Teheran, adopted by the UN International Conference on Human Rights which met there in 1968, which states that the Universal Declaration 'constitutes an obligation for the members of the international community'. Accordingly, it may be argued that, even if it constituted no such obligation when it was adopted in 1948, the member states of the UN changed their minds 20 years later and thenceforth regarded it as binding upon themselves.

Yet another argument, and one which I personally find particularly persuasive, would treat the UN Charter and the Universal Declaration as interconnected documents. Article 55 of the Charter says that 'the United Nations shall promote . . . universal respect for, and observance of, human rights and fundamental freedoms for all without distinction as to race, sex, language, or religion'; and Article 56 adds that 'all Members *pledge themselves* to take joint and separate action . . . for the achievement of the purposes set forth in Article 55' (my italics). The Charter never defined the 'human rights and fundamental freedoms' which the member states of the UN pledged themselves to respect and observe, but the Universal Declaration did, with a clear reference back to that very pledge in its own preamble. Accordingly, so the argument runs, the two instruments must be read together: in the first, which is a binding treaty, the member states pledge themselves to respect and observe X, and if you want to know what X is you will find it fully described in the second – with a reference back to the first, to make it clear that this is precisely what you are intended to do. A variant of this argument would treat the Universal Declaration as an aid to the interpretation of what would otherwise be an ambiguous phrase in the Charter – indeed, the only such aid to be found among other international instruments.[8]

All this is good material for scholarly debate among international lawyers. As more years pass, more sovereign states ratify the global or regional treaties, and even more of them cite the Universal Declaration with approval, and as the International Court of Justice progressively adds more to the few *dicta* on the subject that it has so far pronounced,[9] the weight of the arguments in favour of the Universal Declaration as a law-making instrument will become still greater, until eventually its legal force will be beyond dispute.

The legal position of South Africa

Until we reach that point, there remains a considerable grey area in this field. Perhaps the most important current example is the position of South Africa. The system of racial discrimination practised by that sovereign state under the name of *apartheid* is unreservedly condemned by the entire international community, without a dissenting voice. There can be no question about the moral validity of that condemnation. But, morality apart, is there any *legal* basis for it?

I would suggest an affirmative answer to that question. South Africa is by no means unique in violating the human rights and fundamental freedoms of large numbers of its inhabitants, but what distinguishes it from its fellow culprits in the international community is that it is, so far as I know, the only sovereign state in which racial discrimination is openly institutionalised by its own domestic legal system. There are, as we all know, only too many other states which practise racial discrimination – as there are states which practise censorship of the press, lock up their dissidents on trumped-up charges, persecute members of minority groups, or cause critics of the regime in power to 'disappear'. But one would never be able to guess this simply by reading their national constitutions, or their ordinary domestic laws – all of which would appear, on paper, to give ample protection for the human rights and fundamental freedoms of all their inhabitants.

In this respect, South Africa can escape just one charge which may be rightly levelled at these other states: the charge of hypocrisy. For the South African legal system quite openly discriminates – and discriminates adversely– against millions of the inhabitants of that state, on the single criterion of the colour of their skins. For that reason – that is, because of South Africa's brutal frankness in legalising the racial discrimination which it practises – I would contend that its conduct in this respect is illegal in international law, despite the fact that South Africa has not ratified any of the global or regional human rights treaties.

Put shortly, the argument in support of this proposition goes something like this: South Africa is a state party to the United Nations Charter, which is a legally binding treaty; under Articles 55 and 56 of that Charter she is legally bound 'to take . . . action . . . for the achievement of . . . universal respect for, and observance of, human rights and fundamental freedoms for all without discrimination as to race'; she has signally failed to take any such action, and indeed even the most cursory examination of her laws displays massive 'distinctions as to race'; accordingly, South Africa is in flagrant breach of her obligations under the UN Charter. Note that, for this purpose, there is no need to invoke any other treaty, or even the Universal Declaration: whatever may be the precise definition of 'human rights and fundamental freedoms', the South African legal system distinguishes in respect of them between races, and that is enough.

No more has been attempted here than to sketch out the main steps in this argument. Each of them deserves, and is capable of, far more detailed elaboration. But if one accepts the argument, then one has firm *legal* grounds for condemning South Africa in the international forum, and for taking the measures which international law allows to be taken against law-breakers – including, for example, economic sanctions.

Theory and practice

In a sense, then, the case of South Africa is comparatively simple. But, as we know only too well, violations of human rights are rife in other places too; including, regrettably, states which have ratified the United Nations Covenants, or one of the regional treaties. What conclusions can we derive from this about the degree of acceptance of the new international legal order in matters of human rights?

Some would say that these facts support a negative conclusion. This is the sceptical position held by many, including a number of prominent American lawyers who hold that the United Nations Charter, the Universal Declaration, and the various global and regional treaties which together constitute the international legal code of human rights, have had precious little effect on the actual performance of the states which have subscribed to them; that these things are ultimately governed by the realities of politics and economics; and that, accordingly, the expectations of 1945 were idealistic, impractical, and incapable of realisation. In short, what has been generated since then has been nothing more than a lot of useless (and, some would add, expensive) talk and paper.

There is undoubtedly a good deal of force in that argument. As a matter of empirical fact, gross and persistent violations of human rights continue to be perpetrated all over the world, in countries of almost every political or economic complexion, and almost every stage of development. But it seems to me, for three reasons, to be a little facile to conclude from this that the new legal code has not yet even begun to influence reality.

The first reason is one familiar enough to all historians: we have no control group with which we can compare what has actually happened. We cannot run an experiment in which we could observe a hypothetical world in which the legal developments in this field since 1945 had never taken place, and see whether in those circumstances there would have been no more, or no worse, violations of human rights than those which we have observed in the real world.

The second reason is that the sceptical position is founded on a fallacious view of the function of laws. It is notorious that the city of Chicago has an exceptionally high incidence of murders. But that is surely not a reason for arguing that murder should cease to be a criminal offence under the laws of the state of Illinois, but rather that one should try to find out why the murder rate is so high in that particular city, and what steps could be taken, in addition to the prohibition of the criminal code, to bring it down.

The third reason is an empirical counter-argument: even in the short time that the new legal order has been in force, there is some evidence that it *can* operate as a constraint on violations. The means whereby it achieves this result are complex and indirect, but now demonstrable in several instances. Take, for example, the case of the military regime which came to power by a coup in Greece in 1964. The violations of human rights which that regime perpetrated were such that a number of other European states instituted proceedings against Greece before the European Commission of Human Rights. Those proceedings led to the effective expulsion of Greece from the Council of Europe in December 1969, following findings by the Commission of massive violations of human rights by its government, in breach of its legal obligations under the European Convention.[10] Less than five years later, that government was successfully overthrown by its internal opponents.

But this was not simply a case of *post hoc, ergo propter hoc*: underlying that sequence was an important shift in *legitimacy* from that government to its opponents. The crucial condition for the continued authority of any government over its citizens is its legitimacy, as perceived both by those citizens and by the rest of the international community. Without it, no government can survive for long. Once its legitimacy is called into question, it becomes legitimate for its opponents to seek to overthrow it, and legitimate also for the other states in the international community to give those opponents both moral and material support. I therefore share the view of many that, while the legal condemnation of the Greek colonels' regime by the European Commission of Human Rights may not have been the only cause of their overthrow, it contributed materially to that event.

The same sequence, and in my view the same causative process, may be seen in the eventual overthrow of the Emperor Bokassa of Central Africa, the Shah of Iran, General Amin of Uganda, President Somoza of Nicaragua, President Macias of Equatorial Guinea, the Argentinian, Uruguayan, and Bolivian military juntas and, most recently, President Marcos of the Philippines. I believe that, over the next few years, we shall witness a similar evolution in South Africa, whose government is already seeing itself increasingly deserted by many of its former friends and trading partners, as its legitimacy shrinks visibly in both national and international perceptions, and the legitimacy of its opponents – even that of the African National Congress, despite its explicit adoption of violence as a means for the achievement of its ends – increases in like measure.

Perhaps this is the reason why, with the single remaining exception of South Africa, the traditional riposte of 'inadmissible intervention in the internal affairs of a sovereign state' appears to have gone markedly out of fashion. Today, one hardly ever hears it from any government that is being publicly attacked on its human rights record. Instead, such governments increasingly adopt the technique of what Anglo-Saxon lawyers call 'confession and avoidance'; that is, they attempt to find legal excuses for their actions, such as states of emergency, the exigencies of national security, and justifications on grounds such as public health or public morals. Though the continuance of violations is deplorable, this trend supports a limited degree of optimism, since it entails at least nominal acceptance of the new international order. An accused person who pleads 'not guilty' and enters a formal defence may still be guilty, but at least he accepts the rule of law and the jurisdiction of the court.

Implementation and enforcement

That phrase – 'jurisdiction of the court' – leads me to the next problem area.

The old positivist objection to human rights – that they were, at best, moral claims, but that one could not properly proceed to call them 'rights' until there were at least some laws which made them so – has been met in part by the enactment of laws on the international plane which give rights to individuals. But a more extreme kind of positivist would assert that the use of the word 'rights' cannot be justified until there are not only declared laws, but *enforceable* laws: that is, until the so-called rights can be effectively vindicated by proceedings in a competent court which has the power to enforce its judgments.

This contention needs to be considered on two planes, the national and the international. On the national plane, the question needs to be considered separately for each of the world's sovereign states, and this is a mammoth exercise in comparative law, part of which is in fact being undertaken by the Human Rights Committee in respect of the state parties to the ICCPR, under the reporting procedure established by Article 40 of that treaty; and the new Committee of Experts established by ECOSOC, the United Nations Economic and Social Council, has now begun a parallel task under the ICESCR. Here, the classical division is between states whose legal systems are 'monist' – like most of those of the Roman Law tradition, and also the USA – and whose obligations in international law are therefore 'self-executing' (that is, directly enforceable) in their own courts, provided they are sufficiently clear and specific; and those whose legal systems are 'dualist' – like those of the United Kingdom and most other Anglo-Saxon systems, as well as the Scandinavian nations – whose courts cannot generally apply or enforce international law unless and until it has been 'incorporated' or 'transformed' into domestic law by the national legislature.

But apart from that division, there is also another one between those countries whose governments sincerely wish to comply with their human rights obligations under the treaties they have ratified, and those that do not. There are both monist and dualist countries which fall into each of these categories. The Soviet Union, for example, is technically monist: in theory, its courts could directly enforce the rights of its inhabitants under the Covenants which the Soviet Union has ratified; in practice, one wonders what would be the fate of any Soviet dissident who sought to institute such proceedings. In the opposite corner stand those dualist countries whose governments are genuinely concerned to comply with their obligations under international human rights treaties: their problem is whether this objective can be better achieved by incorporating the text of the treaty itself into domestic law, or by seeking to harmonise each separate branch of that law with the treaty obligations, in the hope that conformity will be better achieved by this route.

The problem is not an easy one, and different countries have sought to resolve it in different ways. Austria, for example, has incorporated the whole of the European Convention on Human Rights into its constitution, with direct access to its constitutional court by every individual who claims to have suffered a violation. At the other end of the spectrum, successive governments of the United Kingdom have so far resisted all pressure to incorporate: instead, they have followed a policy of fighting almost every case, first in the domestic courts, and then all the way through the Strasbourg procedures to the European Court of Human Rights; only when they finally lose there (as they frequently do) do they present a Bill to Parliament in order to try to bring domestic law into conformity with the Convention obligations.

International organs

At the national level, implementation and enforcement of the new international legal order is therefore highly variable around the globe. Sadly, this is also still the position at the international level. So far, the extreme positivist's objections are only fully met by two institutions: the European Court of Human Rights and the Inter-American Court of Human Rights, both of which can render binding judgments[11] against sovereign states condemning them for violating the human rights and fundamental freedoms of individuals, and ordering them to afford 'just satisfaction' or 'fair compensation' to the injured party.[12]

In Europe, this court has now been established for over 30 years, and has developed an increasing degree of authority in that time. Its judgments today command unqualified respect throughout the member states of the Council of Europe (only one of which, Turkey, has not yet accepted its compulsory jurisdiction), and are invariably complied with. The Inter-American Court has only quite recently begun its work, and its compulsory jurisdiction has so far been accepted by only eight of the 19 state parties to the American Convention, but there is no reason to suppose that it will not eventually establish a similar position.

Regrettably, however, this acceptance of the compulsory jurisdiction of international courts in matters of human rights, and the concomitant sacrifice of national sovereignty, is still confined to only a handful out of all the world's sovereign states. Some more of them, 38 at the last count, have ratified the Optional Protocol to the ICCPR, under which individuals may institute formal proceedings before the Human Rights Committee; the outcome of these are 'views' expressed by the Committee, rather than binding judgments, but the states concerned (apart from Uruguay, during the period of the military regime there) generally accept them, and indeed several have already modified their domestic laws in order to comply with them.

Beyond that, international implementation and enforcement is still only a matter of exhortation, diplomatic or economic pressures, or open condemnation in the forum of international public opinion. These can provide no formally valid answers to the objections of the extreme legal positivist, but they should not for that reason be discounted, for their power can be quite substantial.

Given the high value which states generally – and especially those that have only recently achieved their independence – attach to the concept of national sovereignty, it seems unlikely that there will be a great rush in the foreseeable future towards more subjections to the power of international tribunals to render binding judgments against states which have not already taken such a decision. Even so, there is some gradual progress in that direction, albeit at a decidedly slow pace. For example, the African Charter has now entered into force, and under its provisions an African Commission on Human and Peoples' Rights will shortly be established, with jurisdiction to receive complaints from individuals against any of the states which have ratified the Charter, without the need for a specific declaration from them accepting the competence of the Commission to entertain such complaints. True, the Commission is not a court and cannot render binding judgments, but there is no reason to suppose that the state parties to the Charter will not treat its findings and reports with respect, and take at least some of the steps that may be found to be needed in order to remedy any violations which the Commission ascertains. Here, perhaps, a degree of guarded optimism may not be entirely out of place.

However, there are other areas where there is little justification for it. Since the adoption of the Universal Declaration nearly 39 years ago, it has become increasingly clear that effective implementation is only likely to be accepted at a regional level, where nations share a common culture and are willing to trust jurists, commissioners, and judges brought up in that culture to scrutinise complaints brought against them by individuals, and to assess their performance in the field of human rights. Non-communist Europe, Latin America and the Caribbean, and now the African continent, have gradually adopted such regional institutions and procedures, but there remain some major gaps.

The first of these is North America, where the United States resolutely refuses to become a state party to any international human rights treaties. Its opposition is founded on the familiar arguments that it has perfectly good domestic – and indeed constitutional – guarantees for the protection of the civil liberties of its inhabitants, and that it is anyway a federation of states, each of which jealously guards its competence in matters of this kind. But the same might justly be said about Switzerland, which has none the less found it possible to ratify the European Convention, and to submit its domestic affairs to the jurisdiction of the Strasbourg institutions.

Another gap is to be found in Asia, where it has hitherto proved impossible, despite many efforts, to establish a regional human rights treaty, with appropriate regional institutions to interpret and apply it, with tragic results for all too many of the inhabitants of some of the countries of that region. But perhaps the most important gap is that constituted by what one might call the Eurasian socialist bloc: China, the Soviet Union, and the East European members of the Warsaw Pact.

China is currently going through some fundamental political changes which appear to include, among other things, an increasing development of legality and legal procedures; no one could safely foretell today whether this may yet lead towards the protection of individual human rights against the state.

Not entirely dissimilar changes are now taking place in the Soviet Union, which has long subscribed to the notion of 'socialist legality'. In principle, there would seem to be no reason why this great nation, and its socialist allies in Eastern Europe, should not elaborate their own regional, and socialist, convention on human rights and fundamental freedoms, with appropriate regional institutions for its application and enforcement. But the principal difficulty here would seem to be the lack of any tradition of true judicial independence, at all events in the Soviet Union itself. This has nothing to do with socialism: it did not exist under the Czars, nor has it developed since. Indeed, the principle of a separation of powers is expressly rejected by Marxism–Leninism as a 'liberal bourgeois' notion: though the Soviet Union has, by all accounts, an excellent legal system and a perfectly competent judiciary which administers a high standard of criminal and civil justice, this whole system breaks down the moment that there is any 'political' aspect to the case – simply because the courts, like all other institutions, are subject to the directions of the omnipotent Supreme Soviet, which is an entirely political body.

Yet, even here, there are beginning to be some hints that not all Soviet lawyers are entirely happy with this situation, and there is at least the glimmer of a possibility that, in the course of the current reforms, there just might develop the beginnings of a new tradition of judicial independence, not only from the parties to a case, but from the other institutions of government. Were this to happen – and in an extremely conservative country like the Soviet Union, such a process could only be very gradual – there might yet be some hope for the better protection there of human rights: not only the economic and social ones, which on the whole are well protected, but the civil and political ones as well.

A generation gap?

In recent years there has been an increasingly vocal movement, which understandably includes many Marxists but is by no means confined to them, calling for the elaboration of what it calls a 'third generation' of collective human rights (sometimes also called 'solidarity' rights), including new rights to development, to a satisfactory environment, and to peace. It is called the 'third' generation on the assumption – which not every historian would share – that the so-called 'bourgeois' rights, which roughly coincide with the rights that are known today as 'civil and political', formed the first generation of human rights, while the so-called 'socialist' rights, which roughly correspond with those which today we call 'economic, social and cultural', formed the second. On this question, let me confine myself here to outlining some general considerations about the merits of attributing either individuality or collectivity to rights which we call 'human' rights.

When weak human being are oppressed, persecuted, or deprived by those stronger than themselves, it is not unnatural that they should join together for mutual protection and concerted resistance, especially when their oppressors also combine with each other. Without the collective solidarity of trade unions or political parties, little would have been achieved for the improvement of the conditions of their members. It is therefore very understandable that the victims of oppression are apt to see human rights as collective issues, and to claim these rights not only for each of them individually, but also (or even preferentially) for all of them as 'collective' rights.

However, I would contend (in common with many other commentators) that such a formulation of the claim for respect for human rights – and, more particularly, if it seeks an enlargement in this direction of human rights law – presents some insuperable theoretical problems, and also some very practical dangers.

We must first recall that the principal oppressors throughout history have themselves been collectivities in the form of states and their public authorities, as well as collectives (including political parties and even churches) within the state. The single objective of human rights theory, and now of human rights law, has therefore always been to protect weak individuals from the oppression of powerful groups, by giving them 'inalienable' rights which 'inhere' in them as individuals. This explains why all the human rights and fundamental freedoms which the modern international legal code defines and protects are formulated as individual rights or freedoms, using such phrases as 'everyone has the right to' or 'every person has the freedom of'. I must emphasise that this is just as much the case for the 'economic, social and cultural' rights in the code as it is for the 'civil and political' ones. On grounds of fundamental principle as well as grammar, therefore, human rights are individual rights, and not collective rights.

This is not to say that collectivities may not have legal rights. On the plane of domestic law, many do. A collectivity, by definition, is something other than the individual members which compose it; it is an abstract entity recognised by the law (or the culture, or the tradition, or the popular perception) as having a 'personality' of its own. Anglo-Saxon and German lawyers call this a 'juristic person', French ones a *personne morale*, in contrast to a 'physical person'. Examples might include a commercial corporation, a municipal authority, a church, a political party, a trade union, a club, a voluntary association, and indeed any other governmental or non-governmental organisation.

Such a recognition of 'legal personality' is often very convenient. None the less, the ascription of 'personality' to an abstraction is no more than a legal fiction. What a company, a club, a local authority, a church, or a trade union in fact consists of is certain individuals, and the land and other things which they control through the powers which the law allows them to exercise, and will enforce for them if they are disputed. And this is precisely what we mean when we say that the law gives these collectivities certain 'rights', exercisable by the collectivity in virtue of its 'legal personality'.

Though most of the world's domestic legal systems adopt such fictions and, for convenience, ascribe various rights to various collectivities, the only fiction which international law adopts is that of 'the state' as a single entity which is more than the sum of its parts: its land, the things on, over and under it, its teeming inhabitants, and even its government. Though international law may allow rights to collectivities of states in the form of certain inter-governmental organisations (such as the United Nations, its specialised agencies like UNESCO and the ILO, and the European Communities), it does not ascribe any rights to non-governmental collectivities: they are simply not the subjects of international law. What it does do, as the consequence of its recent legal revolution, is to ascribe certain rights to *individuals*, and to impose correlative obligations on their states.

Since those 'human' rights are, by definition, the rights which international law ascribes to all human individuals by virtue of the fact alone that they are human individuals, they cannot of their nature belong to abstract collectivities such as companies, clubs, political parties, churches or trade unions. Indeed, the whole purpose of ascribing 'human' rights to every human being, to protect weak individuals from the strong collectivities which seek to exercise power over them, could be fatally undermined if rights of the same paramount rank were to be allowed to those very collectivities. As Professor Heribert Golsung, who was at the time Director of Human Rights at the Council of Europe, once put it: 'In the final analysis, it is an attempt to make the safeguard of human rights dependent upon *raison d'état*, that elusive concept which has been and still is used so frequently to disguise the most cruel violations of human dignity'.[13]

None the less, the movement for the development of collective human rights persists. It would like to see a number of such rights, which are not yet there,[14] added to the international code. One of the principal contentions on which it relies is that there is already one positive right in the international code which is both 'human' and 'collective' at the same time, namely the 'right of self-determination of peoples'.

The 'Right of Self-determination of Peoples'

Both the UN Covenants, which were adopted in 1966 and entered into force ten years later, begin with an identical provision in the following terms:

1. All peoples have the right of self-determination. By virtue of that right they freely determine their political status and freely pursue their economic, social and cultural development.

2. All peoples may, for their own ends, freely dispose of their natural wealth and resources without prejudice to any obligations arising out of international economic co-operation, based upon the principle of mutual benefit, and international law. In no case may a people be deprived of its own means of subsistence.

3. The States Parties to the present Covenant, including those having responsibility for the administration of Non-self-Governing and Trust Territories, shall promote the realisation of the right of self-determination, and shall respect that right, in conformity with the provisions of the Charter of the United Nations.

Progressive acceptance of this right of self-determination has of course aided the recognition of the legitimacy of the claims of colonial peoples to independence, and has been a potent factor in the decolonisation process, until there are hardly any colonies of the classical form left in today's world; and many of the ones that remain (such as the Falkland Islands) do not wish to change their status, and in fact rely on their peoples' right of self-determination to maintain it.

But what *kind* of a right is this? Since the Covenants are widely regarded as human rights treaties, one might be forgiven for thinking that it is a human right – and, since it is ascribed to the collectivity of a 'people', that it is a collective human right. If that were so, it would indeed be the only right in the entire catalogue that was both 'collective' and 'human' at the same time.

However, if one looks more carefully at the Covenants, it turns out not to be so. They do not in fact describe themselves as treaties about 'human' rights: one says that it deals with 'civil and political' rights, and the other with 'economic, social and cultural' rights. Each of them is divided into a number of Parts. Part 1 of each is identical, and contains the single Article quoted in full above. This is a self-contained statement of the rights of peoples, and of the obligation on states which correlate with those rights. Parts 2 and 3, again self-contained, then spell out the 'human' rights of individuals, and the (different) correlative obligations of states about these. The treaties therefore deal, in one Part, with the collective rights of peoples (which, being declared in identical terms in both of them, are therefore civil, political, economic, social, and cultural); in other Parts, they then deal with the individual human rights of discrete individuals.

In order to avoid any possible misunderstanding, let me make one thing quite clear. I do not in any way oppose, or object to, the right of peoples to self-determination: indeed I welcome it without reservation. Nor would I object to the creation of some more rights of peoples, including especially a right to development, provided it can be properly defined; indeed, I have myself taken some part in the elaboration of such a definition in the international forum.[15] My single concern is that there should be no possibility of confusion between the rights of peoples on the one hand, and the 'human' rights of individuals on the other; and above all that there should never be any possibility of the former ranking at the same paramount level as the latter. If a whole people is oppressed, it is entitled to our fullest support in its legitimate struggle against its oppressors. But neither during that struggle, nor after its successful outcome, does the collectivity of that people have any right to abridge or deny any of the individual human rights and fundamental freedoms of its members – or, dare I say it, even of its oppressors – in the name of that struggle, or for any other cause, however grandly named. In short, in any hierarchy of rights, the rights of peoples (or of any other collectivities) must always be subsidiary to the paramount human rights and freedoms of the individuals that compose them.

Notes and references

This paper draws substantially on one delivered in Copenhagen on 10 December 1986 on the occasion of the inauguration of the new Danish Centre of Human Rights, to whom the author is much indebted for allowing him to reproduce some of the same material here.

1. Lauterpacht, H., *International Law and Human Rights* (1950; reprinted 1968), p. 4.
2. See ICCPR, Article 2(1); ECHR, Article 1; American Convention, Article 1(1); African Charter, Article 1.
3. ICCPR and ICESCR, Article 2(1); ECHR, Article 14; American Convention, Article 1(1); African Charter, Article 2.
4. ICCPR, Article 2(3); ECHR, Article 13; American Convention, Article 25; African Charter, Articles 7(1)(a) and 26.
5. It seems, for example, nothing less than scandalous that, when the promotion and respect for human rights and fundamental freedoms is one of the three principal purposes of its existence as declared in its Charter, the United Nations should today be devoting precisely 0.7 per cent of its programme budget to this purpose – with the result that even the official UN human rights organs have been forced to reduce the frequency and length of their meetings to an almost intolerable degree.
6. Probably the strongest arguments in support of this position were put forward by Lauterpacht several decades ago: see *op. cit.*, Ch. 17, p. 394ff.
7. See, for example, Humphrey, J. P., 'The universal declaration of human rights: its history, impact and juridical character', in *Human Rights: 30 Years after the Universal Declaration* (1979), Ch. I. pp. 21ff.; Waldock, H., ICLQ, Supplementary Publication No. 2, 1965, p. 15.
8. See, in this connection, Article 31 of the Vienna Convention on the Law of Treaties.
9. See the *Genocide Convention Case*, ICJ Reports, 1951, 15; the *Barcelona Traction Case*, ICJ Reports, 1970, 4; the *Namibia Case*, ICJ Reports, 1971, 16; and the *Iranian Hostages Case*, ICJ Reports, 1980, 4.

10. See the Commission's Report in the case of *Denmark, Norway, Sweden and The Netherlands* v. *Greece*, Yearbook of the European Convention on Human Rights, Vol. 12 *bis*.

11. See ECHR, Articles 52 and 53; American Convention, Articles 67 and 68.

12. ECHR, Article 50; American Convention, Article 63(1).

13. *Forum Europe*, 1979, No. 1.

14. Some of them are now included at a regional level, in the African Charter, but are there called peoples' rights rather than human rights.

15. See *Development of Human Rights and the Rule of Law* (1981).

4

Judicial independence and human rights

LORD ELWYN-JONES

I became acutely aware of the close link between the two concepts of judicial independence and human rights in the 1930s when I accepted invitations from the International Association of Democratic Lawyers to attend as an observer a number of trials in Nazi and Fascist courts. Those in Germany were most inappropriately called 'People's Courts', although the German people and their basic human rights were strangers to their proceedings. One of the dramatic moments in the Nuremberg Trial of the Major Nazi War Criminals, in which I was one of the prosecuting counsel, was the showing of a documentary film Goebbels produced for Hitler, of the trial in a 'People's Court' of senior German army officers implicated in the attempted assassination of the Fuhrer in July 1944. It showed the trial judge, Roland Freisler, a creature of the Nazi regime, hurling abuse and insults at the defendants when they tried to address him. To humiliate them their belts and braces had been removed. The contrast with the restraint and dignity of the Nuremberg proceedings and the correct treatment of the defendants there made a powerful impact even on the defendants themselves.

Lord Justice Lawrence, who presided at Nuremberg, had stated the duties of those taking part in opening the proceedings when he said:

The trial which is now about to begin is unique in the history of the jurisprudence of the world and is of supreme importance to millions of people all over the globe. For these reasons there is laid upon everybody who takes part in this trial a solemn responsibility to discharge their duties without fear or favour, in accordance with the sacred principles of law and justice. The Four Signatories having invoked the judicial process, it is the duty of all concerned to see that the trial in no way departs from those principles and traditions which alone give justice its authority and the place it ought to occupy in the affairs of all civilised states.

In a sense it put all of us who took part on trial.

Apart from Nazi Germany, I had other experiences of the fact that the independence of the judiciary is an early casualty of totalitarian regimes. I remember going to Athens in the autumn of 1936, when General Metaxas ruled Greece, to try to help Professor Svolos, Professor of Constitutional

---

This chapter was submitted in 1987.

Law in the University of Athens and President of the Greek Rights of Man, who had been deported in handcuffs to the island of Milos. The power to send him and other like-minded Greeks into exile had been given to a Committee of Security consisting of a Prefect, the Chief of Police and the Public Prosecutor. Until September 1936 there was a right of appeal to the judges of the Greek High Court against the Committee sentences. Thereafter it was permissible to appeal only to the Committee itself on the ground that 'the judges' – and I quote – 'were personalities moved by humanitarian motives, having no contact with reality nor understanding the safety of the state'.

From Athens I went to Rumania where, during the regime of King Carol and Magda Lupescu, there were hundreds of political prisoners. The Rumanian lawyers I met told me they could do little to help them. They were tried by military tribunals. Counsel who defended opponents of the regime – all dubbed Communists no matter what was their political colour – were told they would be disbarred. There again, an independent judiciary and also an independent Bar became targets of an oppressive regime. One of the lawyers who helped me during my investigations in Bucharest was Patrascanu, a courageous young lawyer who risked his own life to save that of others. He survived the last war, but I was appalled to discover later that he had been sentenced to death during a Stalinist upheaval in Rumania. I also heard later that he had received a posthumous rehabilitation. In those days maintaining the independence of the judiciary and of the Bar during a dictatorship was sometimes literally a matter of life and death.

It was to prevent the recurrence of such crushing of human rights that after the war the victorious nations resolved to bring the protection and extension of human rights to the forefront of political and legal action, through the United Nations, regional organisations and domestic legislation.

There grew out of that resolution what Paul Sieghart in his admirable book, *The International Law of Human Rights*, called

a revolution in human affairs comparable with that of 1789, 1848 and 1917, namely the birth of international human rights law embodied in global, regional and specialized treaties to which the governments which signed and ratified them became parties and committed. Their basis is the Rule of Law, the principle which requires that there should be laws which lay down what the state may or may not do and by which one can test whether any power which it claims, or any particular exercise of such power, is legitimate; and a system of Courts independent of every other institution of the state, including the legislators and the executive, which interprets and applies those laws. The total independence of the Judiciary from everyone else is central to the entire concept of the Rule of Law, for the whole point about a law is that it must be upheld impartially and that no-one must therefore be a judge in a cause in which he has any personal interest, or if he is open to illegitimate pressures either overtly or behind the scenes from the friends of either of the parties, – especially if one of them is the state, through its public authorities and its officials and agents.

No less important, as I have already indicated, is an independent legal profession, fearless of appearing against the state on behalf of unpopular clients. Sir Thomas Erskine gave memorable expression to this in 1792 when he was attacked and urged from the highest quarters to return the brief he had accepted for the defence of Tom Paine, who was being prosecuted for publishing his tract called *The Rights of Man*. Erskine wrote:

> From the moment that any advocate can be permitted to say that he will or will not stand between the Crown and the subject arraigned in the Court where he daily sits to practise, from that moment the liberties of England are at an end.

The basic principle is set out in Article 10 of the Universal Declaration of Human Rights:

> Everyone is entitled in full equality to a fair and public hearing, by an independent and impartial tribunal, in the determination of his rights and obligations and of any criminal charge against him.

This is repeated in most of the General Human Rights Treaties like Article 6(1) of the European Convention which the United Kingdom has, of course, signed and ratified and to which it is subject even though it has not incorporated it in its law.

The independence of the judiciary involves both the personal independence of individual judges and the institutional independence (especially the administrative independence) of the courts. As to the former, the oath taken by a judge in England and Wales when he is sworn in by the Lord Chancellor encapsulates the whole duty of a judge. It is that he 'will do right to all manner of people after the laws and usages of this realm without fear or favour, affection or illwill'.

How independent are British judges? Ever since the Act of Settlement of 1701 High Court judges can only be removed by an address by both Houses of Parliament. Only one judge has actually been removed in this way – and that was in 1830. The risk that the British system leaves open the possibility of removing a judge for party political reasons unconnected with his or her ability and impartiality as a judge has not, in fact, materialised. This has been due in great measure to the understanding and respect which both Parliament and the judges – with occasional exceptions – have had for each other's functions and to Parliament's acceptance of the fundamental importance of the need for the judiciary to be independent.

In this process the office of Lord Chancellor has played an important part, because by being Speaker of the House of Lords and also head of the judiciary and a member of the Cabinet, he is able to forestall at an early stage incidents and clashes which could lead to constitutional conflict.

Circuit judges are not so fully safeguarded as High Court judges and can be removed by the Lord Chancellor for misconduct or incapacity. More than once during my term of office I was pressed both by Members of the House of Commons and by the press to remove some Circuit judge or other on more slender grounds than that. An isolated error, an insensitive remark from the Bench, or the passing by a normally sensible judge of a sentence thought to be grossly inadequate, was urged upon me as a ground for his removal. Such isolated grounds for criticism would, in my view, not have justified such a step and indeed would have been an improper interference with the independence of a judge.

This is not to say that public opinion can or should be ignored. Indeed at the present time of increasing crime it is natural and right that the public should concern itself with the problems of law-breaking, what causes them and how they should be dealt with.

There used to be inhibitions about criticising courts and judges, but it is now about half a century since Lord Atkin in a famous speech said: 'No wrong is committed by any member of the public who exercises the ordinary right of criticising, in good faith, in private or public, the public act done in the seat of justice'. He went on to say: 'Justice is not a cloistered virtue; she must be allowed to suffer the scrutiny and respectful, even though outspoken, comments of ordinary men'. He might have added 'and of journalists' who, however, I would not think of dismissing as 'ordinary men'. If judicial independence is to be preserved, three things are, in my view, necessary:

1. Appointment to judicial office must be seen to be based on merit alone and not as a reward for political services rendered.
2. The authority to correct judicial errors must be contained within the judicial system itself and not be performed by Parliament or the government.
3. The judge must be free from pressure to tailor his or her decisions to make them acceptable to the government of the day.

What must not be overlooked in stressing the importance of the independence of the judiciary to the British system of judges is the importance also of trial by jury as guardian of the liberty of the subject and of human rights. In concluding his Hamlyn Lectures on *Trial by Jury* Lord Devlin asserted:

The first object of any tyrant in Whitehall would be to make Parliament utterly subservient to his will and the next to overthrow or diminish trial by jury, for no tyrant could afford to leave a subject's freedom in the hands of twelve of his countrymen. So that trial by jury is more than an instrument of justice and more than one wheel of the constitution. It is the lamp that shows that freedom lives.

If this is so, its light has been greatly dimmed in several former British colonies, like Singapore, which have abolished the right of trial by jury.

Juries are required to bring in verdicts in accordance with the law. They have not always done so. The refusal of juries to convict of certain offences has from time to time been directly responsible for changes in the law. Reluctance of juries to bring in guilty verdicts on a wide range of offences carrying the death penalty resulted in the gradual limitation of their number. When, in my time, murder carried the death penalty, I believe this explained many acquittals of murder in jury trials. In more recent times, it was almost impossible to get a jury to convict of motor manslaughter, so Parliament introduced the offence of 'killing by reckless driving'. It was jury verdicts that increased the pressure on the government to repeal Section 2 of the Official Secrets Act of 1911, which had become almost wholly discredited.

The power of Britain's courts is, as I have indicated, extensive. But it is subject to a fundamental limitation. This ensures the sovereignty of Parliament. Judges cannot challenge an Act of Parliament on the grounds that it is unjust or unconstitutional. As Lord Scarman has said, they must obey it however mischievous they believe it to be. Subject to that major limitation, the law is in the judges' hands. The Common Law rights and duties of the citizen originate in, and are developed by, the decisions of the judges. While there are in English law no constitutional safeguards against the power of the sovereign Parliament, this has not deterred judges from establishing for themselves a strong and, by now, broadly accepted position as the protector of the citizen against the unlawful acts of government. They have done so cautiously, proceeding, as Lord Wright put it, 'from case to case, like the ancient Mediterranean marines, hugging the coast from point to point and avoiding the dangers of the open sea of system and science'. That was written in 1938. The judges have become more adventurous since then.

Britain has seen increasing judicial scrutiny of the activities of the administration, in which the judges have shown a more positive attitude than before. They have, for instance, asserted the power of the court to correct errors of law made by administrative tribunals: *R.* v. *Northumberland Compensation Appeal Tribunal, ex parte Shaw* [1952] 1 KB 338. They have decided that 'ouster' or 'finality' clauses do not protect a decision made outside jurisdiction: *Anisminic Ltd.* v. *Foreign Compensation Commissions* [1969] 2 AC 147. They have extended to all decision-makers the obligation to comply with the basic rules of natural justice, especially a fair hearing and the opportunity to meet charges: *Ridge* v. *Baldwin* [1964] AC 40 (dismissal of Chief Constable by Watch Committee); *Attorney General* v. *Ryan* [1950] AC 718 (citizenship application to Minister).

As Lord Scarman has readily conceded: 'In the protection of human rights the judges in the absence of written constitutional safeguards' (which he himself believes to be necessary now) 'have themselves developed and refined the principles regulating the basic freedoms of the citizen – freedom of speech (including, of course, the printed word), freedom of association, liberty of the person, the integrity and dignity of the human being.' The action for damages for false imprisonment depends upon no enactment, nor does the writ of habeas corpus – by which the courts can release the citizen from unlawful arrest – owe its origin to Parliament. The judges are now developing an administrative law by a process of judicial review of the acts, decisions or omissions of central and local government in its dealings with the citizen. They have used judicial review to break through the old technical procedures and to enable a person complaining of a public authority's infringement of his public law right to obtain a remedy. Although Parliament did incorporate judicial review into the statute law in 1981, the origins and the development of judicial review are the work of the judges. In doing so they have not set out to establish a system of appeals to the courts from administrative decisions. Administration belongs to the government and not to the courts. As Lord Roskill has said: 'Judges cannot and are not qualified to govern and must never attempt to do so. Judicial review is not an appeal from an administrative decision. It is a review by the courts of the manner in which, and the process by which, a particular decision was reached.'

Some would extend judicial power still further and advocate a Bill of Rights, containing entrenched constitutional provisions protecting human rights and the creation of a Supreme Court, by which the constitutionality of ordinary legislation should be judged.

The Lords, in 1977, set up a powerful Select Committee of the House to report on the question whether a Bill of Rights is desirable and if so, what form it should take. Six members of the Committee, in due course, reported in favour and five were against the proposal. But they all accepted that the European Convention, despite its admitted shortcomings, was the only feasible model on which to base a United Kingdom Bill of Rights, if there was to be one. They all agreed also that

in any country, whatever its constitution, the existence or absence of legislation in the nature of a Bill of Rights can, in practice, play only a relatively minor part in the protection of human rights. What is important, above all, is a country's political climate and traditions. . . . The Committee . . . received no evidence that human rights are, in practice, better protected in countries which have a code of fundamental human rights embodied in their law than they are in the United Kingdom.

With this I myself am disposed to agree.

Clearly and rightly, the subject of human rights will not go away. When we debated the Bill of Rights in the House of Lords in 1977 I suggested the possible setting up of a Standing Commission on Human Rights with the ongoing function of revising our law to ensure that it complies with our international obligations on human rights, including the European Convention. I suggested a body independent of the government with the appropriate range of legal and other expertise which would make recommendations to the government. Its reports would be published. If, as I suspect will be the case, the latest version of a Bill of Rights presented to Parliament is not accepted, it may well be worth giving further thought to this idea.

5

The legal protection of refugees

RICHARD PLENDER

The scale of the problem

There is an epidemic in the world which now afflicts more than 12 million people. The numbers are growing at an alarming rate and are now so numerous that states are increasingly unwilling to accept those who suffer from this condition; and the international machinery created to deal with the phenomenon is unequal to the task. The 12 million sufferers are the world's refugees: defined in the Geneva Convention of 1951[1] as those who are outside their countries of nationality and unable or unwilling to avail themselves of the protection of those countries, owing to well-founded fear of being persecuted for reasons of race, religion, nationality, membership of a particular social group or political opinion.

In June 1985, at the height of the Band Aid appeal, there were over 340,000 Eritreans and Tigreans in refugee camps in eastern Sudan. Early in 1986, almost 65,000 of these Ethiopians returned home; but at the same time Ethiopia itself was a place of sanctuary for 130,000 refugees from the Sudan.

The movement of refugees presents logistical problems for aid agencies. In 1980, 250,000 Chadians sought refuge in the Cameroons, Central Africa and the Sudan. Most were repatriated in 1981–82 but again early last year there were more than 100,000 Chadians in the Sudan. In August 1985 2,000 Ugandans returned home from the southern Sudan, following the overthrow of Milton Obote; and in early 1986 these people and more came back to the Sudan, where the government estimates that there are at present a quarter of a million Ugandans. In April that year, 50,000 Ugandans again returned home from the Sudan; not as a result of an improvement in conditions in that country but in consequence of armed attacks on refugee camps established by the United Nations.

In Asia, it is estimated that more than a quarter of the population of Afghanistan has fled to Pakistan and Iran. Indeed, the Islamic Republic of Iran, the source of so many refugees in Europe, has provided asylum to no fewer than two million Afghans. In the Baluchistan region of Pakistan there are more than half a million Afghans: one for every seven native residents. In India, there are some 130,000 Sri Lankan Tamils who have fled the

This chapter was submitted in 1987.

violence of 1984–85, quite apart from those who were 'repatriated' pursuant to the Shastri–Bandaranaike Pacts.[2] The invasion of Cambodia by Vietnamese forces in 1978 forced thousands of refugees into Thailand.

For the United Kingdom, the problem of refugees has assumed particular significance in connection with the Crown colony of Hong Kong. Twelve years ago the attention of the world was fixed on the 'boat people' from Vietnam. Today, they receive less attention; but they are still arriving in Hong Kong, and although their numbers are not as great as they were in 1975, they are rising. In 1985, 1,200 Vietnamese refugees reached Hong Kong. In the first six months of 1986 there were 1,600 arrivals.

The policy currently applied by the government of Hong Kong is officially designated as one of 'humane deterrence'. The policy merits careful scrutiny, for in different forms and in different degrees it is followed in several of the principal destinations of refugees, including the Federal Republic of Germany. The phrase employed by the government of Hong Kong unwittingly expresses that government's dilemma. For those who have fled from persecution, and have not been deterred by the risk of arrest and 're-education', nor by the perils of the China Sea, nor by pirates will scarcely be deterred by governmental treatment that most of us would readily characterise as humane.

Since July 1982 the refugee camps of Hong Kong have been closed. Within those camps there now live approximately 8,500 people. A significant proportion have been there for four years. Every month 20 ethnic Chinese fugitives, who have been in the camps for long periods, are permitted to leave the camps. From time to time other groups are resettled. In late 1985 the United Kingdom accepted 500 others on a basis of family reunion.

The facilities within the camps and the conditions of overcrowding and prospects of resettlement are such that in 1985 1,800 of the boat people arriving in Hong Kong chose to continue their perilous journeys (with fresh supplies of food, water and fuel) rather than submit to the camps' regime. The government is convinced, however, that if conditions in the camps were improved, or the process of resettlement accelerated, the numbers arriving in Hong Kong would grow.

A similar argument has been advanced by the government of the Federal Republic of Germany, when meeting the criticisms advanced by the Office of the United Nations High Commissioner for Refugees against the conditions under which asylum-seekers were housed in that country. The United States has responded in comparable terms to criticisms of its policy of interception of Haitians. New restrictions have been imposed on the admission and condition of asylum-seekers in such countries as Switzerland, Denmark and even Sweden, where Minister Gradin announced new and restrictive proposals. If there is one issue of human rights which demands special attention, if there is one international phenomenon calling for a multilateral response, it is the problem of refugees. In the title of Louise Holborn's book, it is a problem of our time.[3]

The right to enjoy asylum

The most urgent need of a fugitive is a place of refuge. His or her most fundamental right is to be granted asylum. The Universal Declaration of Human Rights[4] addresses this issue in deceptive language. To the inexpert reader there is great comfort in Article 14(1) of that Declaration, which provides that: 'Everyone has the right to seek and enjoy in other countries asylum from persecution.' It seems tolerably clear, however, that the right to enjoy asylum means no more than the right to enjoy it if it is granted. In its original draft, Article 12 of the Universal Declaration (the precursor of Article 14) stated that 'everyone has the right to seek and be granted in other countries asylum from persecution'. That draft was opposed by the United Kingdom, the Commonwealth of Australia and the Kingdom of Saudi Arabia, delegates from those countries arguing that refugees are not admitted under any obligation, and the recognition of a right to be granted asylum would violate state sovereignty. The wording was amended accordingly; and the amendment provoked Sir Hersch Lauterpacht's rebuke that it made the article 'artificial to the point of flippancy'.

In the resolution establishing the Office of the United Nations High Commissioner for Refugees,[6] the General Assembly called upon states to co-operate with the High Commissioner, notably by admitting refugees; but neither that resolution nor the Geneva Convention on the Status of Refugees went so far as to create a right to receive asylum. The Conference of Plenipotentiaries at which the Convention of 1951 was drafted included in its minutes the recommendation 'that governments continue to receive refugees in their territories and that they act in concert in a true spirit of international co-operation, in order that these refugees may find asylum and the possibility of resettlement'. The language is stirring: but the legal force of such a recommendation is meagre.

In 1977 the United Nations convened a conference on Territorial Asylum at which a draft Convention was debated.[7] One item envisaged that contracting states would be under an obligation to 'use their best endeavours to ensure non-rejection of asylum-seekers at the frontier'. Even that provision proved controversial. Some states called for the substitution of the word 'endeavour' for 'use best endeavours', which seems to imply that states should try, but need not try very hard. Others called for the deletion of the article altogether. In the event, the negotiations proved abortive. Dr Weis wrote the epitaph of the Conference:

It seems unlikely that a Convention on Territorial Asylum which constituted
progress from the legal and humanitarian angles could be concluded in the
near future on a universal level . . . and still less that it would be widely
ratified.

It is tempting, therefore, to deny the existence of a right to asylum, and
even to respond in terms of disenchantment to the international community's
pronouncements on the subject. To yield to that temptation is both imprudent
and destructive. Article 14 of the Universal Declaration of Human Rights,
which speaks of the right to enjoy asylum, has to be interpreted in the light
of the instrument as a whole; and must by taken to mean something. It implies
that although an asylum-seeker has no right to be granted admission to a
foreign state, equally a state which has granted him asylum must not later
return him to the country whence he came. Moreover, the Article carries
considerable moral authority and embodies the legal prerequisite of regional
declarations and instruments.

It proved to be the inspiration for the General Assembly's Declaration on
Territorial Asylum of 1967,[9] which yields support for the view that the principle of *non-refoulement* has matured into a principle of customary international law. That Declaration refers in its preamble to Article 14(1) of the
Universal Declaration; and states in the text that persons entitled to invoke
that Article of the Declaration shall not be subjected to measures such as
rejection at the frontier, expulsion or compulsory return to any state where
they may be subjected to persecution.

Furthermore, the Universal Declaration of Human Rights provided
in Article 14 a model for regional affirmations of the right to enjoy asylum.
It is true that in Europe the Universal Declaration has had relatively
little direct influence in this respect. The European Convention on Human
Rights[10] is silent on the right of asylum (although this has not prevented the
Commission from addressing the situation of refugees in the context of other
provisions) and the Council of Europe's Declaration on Territorial Asylum
dated 1977[11] is a relatively tame document which reaffirms the states' right
to grant asylum and their intention to maintain their liberal attitude on the
subject. The American Convention of Human Rights, or Pact of San Jose,[12]
goes further. It states that

Everyone has the right to seek and be granted asylum in a foreign territory,
in accordance with the legislation of the state and international conventions,
in the event he is being pursued for political offences or related common
crimes.

Moreover, the Declaration on Refugees adopted at Cartagena in November
1984[13] provides a comprehensive framework for the protection of refugees,
including fugitives from violence, conflicts and mass violations of human
rights. The African Convention on Refugees of 1969[14] goes even further.

Using the same language as was prepared for the United Nations' Draft Convention on Territorial Asylum, it proclaims that member states shall

> use their best endeavours, consistent with their respective legislations, to receive refugees and to secure the settlement of those refugees who, for well-founded reasons, are unable or unwilling to return to their country of origin or nationality.

From these developments we may draw two conclusions. The first is that the right to be granted asylum does not exist as a right protected by customary or conventional international law, even at the regional level. The second is that the right to enjoy asylum is not hollow or imaginary: it has a real and significant content in the case of the person to whom asylum is granted, for it constitutes a guarantee that his status will not be withdrawn. Moreover, the inchoate right to be granted asylum, which finds expression in the Pact of San Jose and in the OAU Convention, is of great but indirect value to the asylum-seeker. At the least, these regional instruments strengthen the hands of governments disposed to grant asylum, by enabling them to respond to their neighbours' criticisms. Indeed, the regional Conventions avoid the use of the word 'persecution'.

The principle of non-refoulement

The guarantee that asylum will not be withdrawn is expressed and amplified in the famous Article 33 of the Geneva Convention on the Legal Status of Refugees. This provides that no contracting state shall expel or return (refouler) a refugee in any manner whatsoever to the frontiers of territories where his life or freedom would be threatened on account of his race, religion, nationality, membership of a particular social group or political opinion. That Article presents serious interpretative difficulties, to which we shall give attention: and in recent years it has been the subject of a wider controversy. The debate is over the question whether the principle embodied in Article 33 represents a rule of general international law, binding on parties to the Convention and on non-parties. The debate raises a fundamental issue, since only two-thirds of the world's states are parties to the Convention.

Only ten years ago Prince Sadruddin Aga Khan, as United Nations High Commissioner for Refugees, observed in his Hague lectures[15] that the rule against rejection of refugees at the frontier is not accepted by all states. Professor Grahl-Madsen, writing in 1980, reached the conclusion that non-refoulement has not matured into a rule of customary international law,[16] and his conclusion was echoed by Dr Kalin in 1982.[17] It seems to me, however, that modern practice affords a basis for a more optimistic assessment; and I am gratified to see that my conclusion is shared by Dr Goodwin-Gill.

Evidence that the principle has matured into a rule of general international law is available from many sources: from treaties ancillary or subsequent to the Geneva Convention, in particular Article 11 of the OAU Convention of 1969; from formal international pronouncements including the Declaration on Territorial Asylum of 1967; from public pronouncements of offices of state, including those made at the Geneva Conference of 1977; and from a remarkable congruence of domestic law, so striking that a rapporteur at a colloquy held in Heidelberg in 1985 was able to summarise the reports of 62 participating states as follows:

> In all countries, even persons still being at the frontier seem to be protected against refoulement to a country where their lives or freedom would be threatened . . .[19]

Indeed, the report of the thirty-third session of the UNHCR Executive Committee in October 1982 went so far as to refer to the principle of *non-refoulement* as a 'peremptory rule of international law'.

I conclude that the return of a refugee to a territory in which he has a well-founded fear of persecution amounts to a breach of general international law. That rule of law is binding on all states, whether or not parties to the Convention: and in states in which an individual can rely upon customary law but not on an unincorporated treaty, the individual can rely on the principle to which I have referred.

The application of this principle nevertheless gives rise to persistent difficulties. The first problem is that of knowing when '*refoulement*' occurs. Does it arise when the alien presents himself at a frontier seeking admission: or must he be admitted before he is immune from reconduction to his place of origin? Does *refoulement* occur when an asylum-seeker arriving in a small boat is returned not to his country of origin but to the high seas? Does it occur when a public vessel on the high seas refuses to rescue refugees on a small boat, whose occupants are then faced with a choice between returning to persecution and risking their lives at sea? Such questions arise in the daily practice of those concerned with the protection of refugees. That this is so is a testament not only to the gravity of the present problem but also to the inadequacy of the 1951 Convention in the face of the modern volume and character of the flood of refugees.

I must essay answers to the questions that I have posed; but must acknowledge that the case law is sparse and inconsistent and the points controversial. In my view *refoulement* occurs, contrary to the Convention and contrary to customary international law, when a refugee who presents himself at the frontier is denied admission and forced thereby to face persecution in his country of origin. I appreciate that this entails qualifying the general principle of international law whereby each state is free to refuse admission to aliens; but my construction accords with practice and with the purpose of the rule against *refoulement*: and so far as the Geneva Convention is concerned, my construction is supported by the text. Article 32 prohibits the expulsion of aliens 'unlawfully' present in the territory of contracting states, whereas Article 33 prohibits their *refoulement*. The implication is clear: the prohibition of *refoulement* extends to those who are not lawfully in the territory of contracting states, including those who are not in that territory at all.

As for the practice of returning asylum-seekers to the high seas, I am bound to state that the policy, although inhumane, appears not to be inconsistent with the Geneva Convention. Cases may arise in which a refusal to admit asylum-seekers arriving by vessel amounts to the return of these individuals to their country of origin, given the extended meaning of the word 'return' in Article 33 of the Geneva Convention. Save in these exceptional cases, however, the Convention is silent; and the response of the international community to the practice adopted by certain South East Asian states to Vietnamese asylum-seekers in 1982 does not support the view that those states' actions are unlawful.

A similar conclusion must be offered in the case of the interception of a boat by a public vessel on the high seas. We know from recent experience that refugees aboard such boats are by no means invariably rescued by the larger ships plying the seas in the principal regions in which refugees are to be found. The Geneva Convention of 1951, framed with the object of addressing the problem of East European refugees travelling to the West, is unsuited to the case of the so-called boat people; and affords no basis for arguing that there is a legal obligation to rescue them. It is just possible that different considerations apply in the case of the European Convention on Human Rights; for it can be contended that a person is 'within the jurisdiction of a state' when he is in a small vessel on the high seas and at the mercy of a public vessel of that state. The difficulties presented by this argument are, perhaps, too obvious to require elaboration; but in the case of the Geneva Convention the difficulties are even more formidable than in the case of the Europe Convention on Human Rights. For the Geneva Convention prohibits only *refoulement*, and not other forms of inhuman treatment.

The definition of a refugee

If there is one issue on which the Geneva Convention has proved influential, other than in formalising the principle of *non-refoulement*, it is in supplying a definition of a refugee. A refugee is a person outside his country of origin and unwilling or unable to return to it owing to wellfounded fear of being persecuted for any of the reasons given earlier. Thus the Convention protects only fugitives from persecution, by contrast with the more modern Convention adopted under the auspices of the OAU. The latter extends also to 'every person who, owing to external aggression, occupation, foreign domination or events seriously disturbing public order in either part or the whole of his country of origin or nationality, is compelled to leave his place of habitual residence in order to seek refuge'. Thus, fugitives from the dangers caused by war, civic strife, enemy occupation and communal violence are in principle outside the compass of the Geneva Convention as are persons displaced by famines, earthquakes, floods and the events blasphemously described as 'acts of God', such as eruptions of poisoned gas and plagues of locusts.

National courts and tribunals in the states parties to the Geneva Convention are commonly called upon to interpret the definition of 'refugee' contrived in that treaty. Indeed, in the United Kingdom, the only part of the Convention which may be taken to be incorporated into domestic law is the definition.[20] Since the definition tends to exclude from its protection individuals who are in fear of immediate bodily injury in the event of their repatriation, there is a natural tendency to interpret it extensively. That tendency has a certain basis in the preamble to the Convention, which refers to the expression of hope by the Conference of Plenipotentiaries that the Convention will have value as an example exceeding its contractual scope.

Thus, in *Kazie* v. *Home Secretary*[21] a tribunal in the United Kingdom held that an individual has a well-founded fear within the meaning of the Convention when he established 'a serious possibility' of persecution: and in the subsequent litigation in the House of Lords[22] the proposition was restated: 'There must be a "reasonable degree of likelihood" of persecution'. In the United States the courts have required a 'realistic likelihood' of such treatment.[23] Swiss law does not require proof of persecution but of any threat to life, limb or liberty or any other measure entailing intolerable psychological pressure.[24] The term 'race' is construed in the broadest sense. According to the Canadian Immigration Manual it embraces the social concept of race including membership of 'a particular tribe or minority'. The term 'nationality' is taken to mean not only citizenship in its legal sense but membership of any ethnic or linguistic group. The expression 'social group' appears broad enough to encompass those persecuted on account of sexual disposition or behaviour, such as women who are liable to be persecuted for transgressing the social mores of their countries of origin.[25]

Nevertheless, even a liberal interpretation of the Geneva Convention (which is not always to be obtained, at a time of recession and economic stringency) is apt to leave unprotected those who face persecution for engaging in activities contrary to the law of the country of origin, even when those activities were undertaken in consequence of the fugitive's political opinion, race, religion or membership of a particular social group. Two problems are recurrent: those of *Republikflucht* and conscientious objection.

By *Republikflucht* is meant punishment for unauthorised stay abroad. Penalties for unauthorised foreign travel or residence are commonly imposed in the laws of the People's Democracies of Eastern Europe: as for example, by Article 101 of the Bulgarian Penal Code of 1968, and Articles 83–84 of the Soviet Criminal Code. Certain of the decisions of the United Kingdom's Immigration Appeal Tribunal suggest that fear of punishment for *Republikflucht* is not fear of persecution within the meaning of the Convention, since the law of the state of origin applies indiscriminately to persons of all religions, political opinions and social origins: moreover, a person cannot be said to be unwilling to return to his country of origin for reason of fear of persecution when in fact he faces prosecution by reason of his unwillingness to return.[26]

It is noteworthy that the courts of the Federal Republic of Germany have taken a less restrictive view of this matter than those of the United Kingdom. Their reasons for doing so are plain: and influenced in part by Article 16(2) of the Basic Law, which provides: '*Politisch verfolge geriessen Asylerecht*': those persecuted for political reason have the right to be granted asylum. Thus, in *Klager*,[27] the Bundesveruraltungsgericht held, in 1971, that punishment for *Republikflucht* was always persecution for reason of political opinion as the purpose of the law was to secure the political sovereign authority of Communism.

In the case of conscientious objection, the case law of the Contracting states is equally inconsistent. In *Doonetas* v. *Home Secretary*[28] the Immigration Appeal Tribunal considered the case of a Jehovah's Witness who faced several long successive periods of imprisonment for refusal to engage in military service. His refusal was an expression of his religious faith but Article 13 of the Greek Constitution provided expressly that no person shall be discharged from fulfilling his obligations to the state by reason of religious conviction. The tribunal considered that the sort of sentences being imposed in Greece for refusal of military service amount to persecution but that persecution was not 'for reasons of religion or political opinion'. The law was not designed with the object of penalising Jehovah's Witnesses; and sentences similar to those imposed on Jehovah's Witnesses were imposed on other conscientious objectors. The decision in *Doonetas* is to be contrasted with that in *Church*,[29] where the fugitive had fled South Africa to avoid being conscripted into the South African security forces. In *Church* the fugitive qualified as a refugee because he had conscientious objections to a particular policy pursued by the South African government; and those objections were an expression of political opinion.

Conclusion

These reflections on the human rights of refugees may provoke the conclusion that they are protected only imperfectly. The principal legal instrument governing their status was designed to deal with those fleeing in smaller numbers, between opposed political ideologies, at a time of economic reconstruction.

Its terms are inapt to deal with the modern wave of refugees from Africa and Asia, more commonly victims of violence than of persecution and arriving in the territories of states parties by means unforeseen in 1951. The paradox is that only the circumstances existing 35 years ago could create the political will needed for the conclusion of an international agreement on the status of refugees. The political circumstances are absent today, but the refugees are with us.

Notes and references

1. Convention Relating to the Status of Refugees, 28 July 1951, 189 UNTS 150.
2. 30 October 1964 (unpublished).
3. L. Holborn, *Refugees: A Problem of Our Time* (1975).
4. New York, 10 December 1948, 42 AJIL (Supp.) 127.
5. Quoted by P. Weis in 50 BYIL (1979) at 151.
6. Res. 428 (v) 1950.
7. See P. Weis, 'Draft United Nations Convention on Territorial Asylum', 50 BYIL (151); R. Plender, 'Admission of Refugees: Draft Convention on Territorial Asylum', 15 *San Diego Law Review* (1979), p. 45.
8. Ibid., p. 169. See further P. Weis, 'The United Nations Declaration on Territorial Asylum', 7 Can YBIL (1969) 92.
9. 14 December 1967, UNGA Res. 2312 (xxii).
10. Rome, 4 November 1950, 213 UNTS 223.
11. Strasbourg, 18 November 1977; Plender, *Basic Documents on International Migration Law* (1988), p. 140.
12. San Jose, 22 November 1969, 9 ILM (1970) 673.
13. See the author's *International Migration Law* (2nd edn, 1988), p. 399.
14. Convention Governing Specific Aspects of the Refugee Problem in Africa, Addis Ababa, 10 September 1969, 1001 UNTS 46.
15. H. H. Prince Sadruddin Aga Khan, 'Legal Problems Relating to Refugees and Displaced Persons', 149 *Hague Recueil*, (1976–I) 287.
16. A. Grahl-Madsen, *Territorial Asylum* (1980), p. 43.
17. W. Kalin, *Das Prinzip der Non-Refoulement* (1982).
18. G. Goodwin-Gill, *The Refugee in International Law* (1983).
19. *Die Rechtsstellung von Ausländern nach staatlicher Recht und Völkerrecht* (1986).
20. Statement of Immigration Rules, HC 169 paras. 73, 134, 165.
21. [1984] Imm. AR 10.
22. *R. v. Secretary of State for the Home Department ex parte Sirakumaran* [1988] 1 All ER 193.
23. *INS Stevic* (1984) 467 US 407; *INS* v. *Cardoza*–Fonseca (1987) 94 L Ed Zd 434.
24. *Loi sur l'asile*, 5 October 1979, FF 1979 II 997.
25. See the authorities set out in the author's *International Migration Law* (2nd edn, 1988), pp. 419–24.
26. *Church* v. *Home Secretary*, 16 March 1982, TH/69153/80 (2288); *Doonetas* v. *Home Secretary*, 14 October 1976, TH/12339/TS (820).
27. 26 October 1971, B. Verw. GE Bd. 39 No. 6.
28. *Supra*, n. 26.
29. *Supra*, n. 26.

6

The right to a fair trial under the European Convention on Human Rights

HENRY SCHERMERS

Article 6 of the European Convention on Human Rights, containing the right to a fair trial, is the Article most frequently invoked. It is also the Article against which the European Commission has found by far the most frequent violations. The Article contains several elements in its drafting upon which one might expect – and I did expect before I joined the Commission – there to be a great diversity of opinion upon their meaning. There are 21 legal systems involved, but it is a remarkable fact that there is so much uniformity in Europe in the thinking about what a fair trial involves.

A fair trial as we understand it may seem strange to people from those countries, particularly in Asia, where they have a different approach: when we hold a civil trial that means 'one party wins, the other party loses'; but in several Asian legal systems it is a middle road that is looked for – when two quarrel, both are in some respects in the right. So it is not to be taken for granted that the idea of a fair trial should be uniform throughout Europe. However, one does feel when entering the Human Rights Commission that there is a common legal culture in Western Europe. Of course there are divergences inside the Commission, but they are not along the lines of nationality. They are far more along the lines of personality, as some people are more conservative while others are more progressive.

The scope of Article 6

One problem which is central to Article 6 is the question: to what kinds of dispute is the Article applicable? The Article provides that it is applicable in the determination of civil rights and obligations or in the case of a criminal charge. The question then arises: what about administrative law? The texts of the Treaty are not completely similar. In the English text fair trial is guaranteed in the determination of 'civil rights and obligations or of any criminal charge'. In the French text it says: 'Everybody has a right that his case be fairly heard in public and within a reasonable time by an independent and impartial tribunal established by law, which decides either a dispute on

This chapter was submitted in 1988.

civil rights and obligations or the well-foundedness of any penal accusation against him'. In the French text there is less emphasis on the limitation to civil and penal law cases.

In earlier drafts of the Article the French text was the same as it is now, but the English text read: 'in the determination of any criminal charge against him, or of his rights and obligations in a suit of law'. Without any discussion, at least not anywhere to be found in the records, that was changed in one of the last drafts, probably to adapt it better to the French text. This leaves us with a number of problems. Does the Convention apply to a right to be released on probation? To a refusal to enter a country? To the right of an alien to reside in a country? Permits? Licences? Diplomas? All those fields may be of great importance for a person, but are not really covered by the notion 'civil rights and obligations'.

The Commission traditionally has been rather restrictive in its approach to this problem. The Commission has for a long time taken the view that all administrative law disputes should remain outside the Convention, because it was intended to be outside the Convention and also because of a fear that including too many kinds of disputes would lead to a watering-down of the requirements. For instance, it is customary in the vast majority of the member states that tax cases are not heard in public. If one is to include tax cases in Article 6 then very likely the requirement that *all* trials have to be public would be weakened. There would be too many examples of cases which need not be public, and this might then finally lead to the submission that Article 6 does not really require publicity. That might then affect the normal civil and penal cases.

Apart from the fear that too wide a scope of the Article would affect the impact of the Treaty provision, there also was a fear that the member states might not be willing to follow the Commission as they did not want administrative law to be included in the Article. The Commission and the Court have no real executive power of any kind; we need to build on the goodwill of public opinion and of the member states. If we antagonise them too much that might in the long run have a detrimental effect on the application of the decisions of the Court and Commission.

Unlike the Commission, the Court has been more progressive. It is willing to bring under the Article all disputes which have an effect of a civil nature, on a citizen's possessions, or on his or her civil status. The Koenig case, the Benthem case and the Feldbrugge case are examples where the Commission was reluctant, but the Court ruled that the proceedings came under Article 6 because they affected a person in his or her civil capacities.

'Contestation' is the French word where the English text uses the word 'dispute'. 'Contestation' is placed by the Court at a central place. Whenever the 'contestation' has civil law aspects, then it can be brought under the Article.

'Contestation' covers all proceedings, the result of which is decisive for private rights and obligations. That means not only private law disputes between individuals, but all disputes between individuals and their state where the outcome is decisive for rights and obligations of a civil nature. The sort of right involved, whether it is civil, commercial or administrative in the description of the national legal order, is not decisive. Nor is the kind of authority making the decision decisive. Thus an organ bearing a name different from the name of a court may still be covered by the Article and will then have to fulfil the requirements of Article 6.

Over the years quite a large group of fields have been identified which have been kept out of the Article, but we never know what developments may occur. All procedures of a fiscal nature have been kept out of Article 6 for a long time and most of them are still considered to be out, but recently a few cases where the Commission considered a fiscal fine as of a penal nature have been brought under the Article. It happens in many countries that a person who does not fill out his tax forms in the correct way has to pay more than the normal amount of taxes. That more (the extra payment) was considered by the Commission as a fine, which made the higher charge of a criminal nature. This created case law where fiscal cases were covered by Article 6, but otherwise tax proceedings are always kept out of the Article.

On many other issues the Commission has restricted the applicability of Article 6. The Article does not cover the execution of judgments, nor is there a civil right to a retrial, to provisional release of prisoners, or to review of detentions. Police investigation is a difficult field. To some extent that comes into criminal proceedings, but so far it has mainly been kept out. Also the deportation of aliens, as a procedure, has been left out of Article 6. Questions of citizenship, constitutional rights, employment benefits to some extent, war victims pensions – many of such fields have been kept out of the Article.

Many people in Strasbourg believe that Article 6 should simply apply to all court proceedings, and that it makes no sense to say that one case is administrative and so there is no right to a fair trial, and another is civil and so the person affected does have a right to a fair trial. My understanding is that governments are now discussing the possibility of adding a new Article to the Convention, an Article 6A for administrative law cases. If this comes about then Article 6 and the new Article together would cover almost all court proceedings. That may be a way out, but then no doubt we will have problems of borderlines if these Articles 6 and 6A differ. Then the Commission would have to decide whether a specific case is covered by the one or the other. It would of course be easier if the same Article could apply to all proceedings.

For the remainder of my paper, I now turn to some specific problems that have arisen. These include matters relating to independence of the court from the investigation process, access to a court, unreasonable delay in a court's decision, independence of the court from government, the anonymity of witnesses, and extradition.

Independence from the investigation

The Commission and the Court have decided that the investigating judge, and the court that finally decides, must not be the same. When a suspect comes before the court he should not meet the judge who investigated his case and already formed an opinion about his guilt. That seems a logical rule, because the judge has to be completely independent. Two problems were probably not foreseen when this ruling was made.

First, there is in child psychology a strong conviction that one should not confront a young child with too many different people. It would be better for the child if there were one children's judge talking to him or her throughout the whole proceedings. In other words, it would be better for the child to have the investigating judge and the judge finally deciding being the same person. Whether this is true or not, it is an argument one should take into account in children's cases. Of course, if it affects the independence of the court finally deciding, a child has the same human right to an independent court as anybody else. But the effect of the decision which requires that it should not be the same person is certainly different in children's cases than it is in other cases.

Then another problem arising is that of Iceland and Denmark, where the court structure differs from that in most other European states. In the Netherlands, for example, only large cities have their own courts and the neighbouring towns go to one of those cities. In the Danish system, by contrast, there is a judge in every large village. The Danes have very many courts, the idea being that the distance between the population and the courts must be small. If the judge lives next door, if you meet the judge all the time in your own village, if you know him well, then it is easier to go to court. But of course a side-effect of this is that the Danish courts are very small. Many of the Danish courts consist of one or two people, and if you have a court of one or two people then the separation between the judge who has to supervise the investigation and the judge who finally decides becomes much more difficult. In Iceland there is a similar problem. In the towns outside Reykjavik there may be only one judge. If he is at the same time the head of the police, then problems in penal law cases may easily arise.

My personal opinion is that the independence of the court should be given priority in all cases of doubt. But so far as it is possible, we have to take account of the other arguments.

Access to a court

Another problem is the recent tendency for courts to become over-burdened. Litigation has become easier, and a major reason for this has been that one can now insure oneself against the legal costs involved. A person who is insured litigates at the expense of the insurance company. This has removed what in the past was a great disincentive from going to law. This increase in business in legal expenses insurance has thus created an increase in the number of disputes being brought before the courts. The increase in litigation has led to the courts becoming over-burdened.

This leads to length of procedure problems. In some countries cases may take three, four, five years before they are decided. That is unacceptable. In such cases we find a violation of the Convention, but that is not enough. Some reparation has to be made. One possible remedy is to appoint more judges, but that costs money. Another solution some states have found is to make appeals more difficult. In several countries an appeal which is held to be without foundation, and an abuse of the court, may lead to a fine.

We recently had a case arising from a dispute on the sale of a house. There were ornaments in the house which were loosely attached to the walls, and it was not clear whether they belonged to the furniture or to the house itself. When the person who was in the house left and wanted to take these ornaments, the man who had bought the house argued the ornaments belonged to it and had passed into his ownership. In the first instance the court decided that the ornaments belonged to the house; on appeal the court decided that they did not belong to the house. The buyer then appealed once more and heard that this was an abuse of the court and that he had to pay a large fine. Was that reasonable? When is it reasonable to require a fine of a person who appeals, if the law permits an appeal? On the one hand it should be possible to prevent appeals which are an abuse of the court; on the other hand we have to be careful that there must be sufficient access to the courts.

There are other problems concerning access to the court. Does it affect access to the courts if a *cautio judicatum solvi* is required? The *cautio* is a certain amount of money which one has to pay before one is admitted to the court, to ensure that the costs of the proceedings can be covered. One will receive this *cautio* back if one wins the case, but the *cautio* is lost when the case is lost. In the past the *cautio* was a rather normal part of litigation and in several legal systems it is still required of foreigners unless it is abandoned in a treaty, which often is the case. Is this a limitation of the right of access to the court? Is it therefore contrary to the Convention to require people to pay a sum of money before they are entitled to litigate? Of course this will depend very largely on the precise facts of each case. If one can litigate only upon payment of £1,000,000 into court, then it is certainly a barrier to access to the court. If it is a small sum of money, it may be acceptable.

High costs of litigation can be a barrier to the access to the court. In penal law you always have the right to free legal assistance if you cannot pay. But in civil law there is no such rule. If you cannot pay you cannot sue. But, if an important interest is at stake, surely one should have a right to free legal assistance. Such a right does exist in most member states. In the *Airey* case[1] the Human Rights Court in Strasbourg ruled that in particular circumstances the right of access to a court may entail a right to free legal aid, even in civil law cases.

In defamation proceedings in the United Kingdom legal aid is never possible. Is that rule too strict? Is it correct that a person who cannot afford to pay for his legal costs himself should be prevented from suing in a defamation case even if he can obviously win? Is it correct that he should *never* receive any legal aid? I leave the question open. Again each case will vary according to its precise factual situation, but a *categorical* exclusion seems undesirable.

When the decision is too late

The Convention provides that a court decision must be reached within a reasonable time. In some states – notably West Germany – the courts strictly enforce this principle. If ligation has taken too long the person charged of a criminal offence is released, even in cases where it is rather obvious that he committed the crime. However, the German courts usually require him to pay his own legal costs.

An accused may also be discharged where he has been found guilty in the first instance, but then appellate proceedings have taken too long. Should this discharge entail that all his costs are compensated and that he even may claim damages because he is to be presumed innocent in the absence of a final decision establishing his guilt? Particularly from Germany and Austria there have been several cases where it seemed obvious that the person was guilty but there was no final court decision establishing this. Should we then not consider that person innocent and believe that as a consequence of that he should be free of all costs?

The independence of the court

Another recent problem has arisen in the requirement that courts must be independent. In one of the European legal systems the law provides for special labour courts. However, when that state's parliament enacted that law it was not clear whether these labour courts were really needed and whether there would be sufficient cases for them. Consequently, not wanting to create more courts than necessary, the parliament accepted the establishment of the courts in principle and empowered the Minister of Justice to establish them as soon as there were sufficient cases. Are these courts there fully 'independent'? One applicant who was involved in litigation with the Minister of Justice in a social security case argued that a newly established labour court was insufficiently independent as it depended for its existence on a decision of the Minister of Justice. In the event the Commission declared the case to be inadmissible because we thought that this was not a kind of dependence that would affect the litigation. But this example serves to illustrate that the ostensibly clear provision of Article 6 that courts should be independent does have its grey areas, and that even the principle of independence is not always clear.

Anonymous witnesses

The issue of anonymity of witnesses in legal proceedings poses enormous difficulties which were raised in a recent case from the Netherlands.[2] In many parts of Europe we are confronted with well-organised crime. There are drug dealers in consortia which are very strong, there are traders in women and children, there are bank robbers, militant anarchist groups, and many different kinds of organised groups of criminals. It is extremely difficult to find witnesses willing to give evidence against members of such groups. There are statistics from the United States indicating that one in every ten murders committed in the United States had something to do with witnesses: either the person was killed in order to prevent him from witnessing, or in revenge for the fact that he did witness. The net result is that in a petty crime the proof is relatively easy, but in a really bad crime there are extreme difficulties in securing the necessary proof. This is one of the reasons why Mafia organisations can live so long.

Therefore there is a strong view that one should accept anonymous witnesses, and allow witnesses simply to make statements to the police. The police report may then be produced in court as proof, except of course if the court is not convinced that the anonymous witnesses are reliable. Unless we do this, professional crime may go on and we must help the police catch the big drug dealers, bank robbers and so on. But that is just one side of the coin. The other side is that these anonymous witnesses by definition are risky. They may be other criminals who want to get rid of a certain person, by making false testimony against him. If you cannot cross-examine such a witness then it may be difficult to find out that he is a false witness. Anonymous witnesses are therefore less secure. A witness, of course, is never absolutely secure but there is more security, more reliability, if there is open discussion in court. Furthermore it is a strong rule in Article 6 that court proceedings should be in the open. If we start lifting these strict rules where do we end? It is better to have two bad criminals walking loose than to have one innocent man in jail.

Which of these two arguments should prevail? Some people believe we must catch the criminals and not be too strict in applying Article 6. Others believe the essential elements of a fair trial must always be complied with.

Extradition

A final problem to be considered relates to extradition and the integration of Europe. If a criminal is lawfully convicted in Milan and subsequently caught in Messina, then he is brought to prison in Milan and punished. If the same man is caught in France, then extradition procedures are needed and under the extradition procedure he can invoke Article 6. The extradition is only possible if it is in accordance with the law, and the procedures involved are lengthy and time-consuming. However, if the procedures are not followed and the man is extradited by the local police not according to French rules, then that is contrary to French law and automatically contrary to the Convention. Is this principle justified in an integrated Europe? Is it acceptable that a person caught in another member state of the Council of Europe should have more rights and protection than a person caught in his own home country? This is an important question, for after 1992 (when the borders become completely open) the criminal after committing the crime – for example in the Netherlands – can easily go to Germany and settle down there. He will then receive extra protection under the extradition rules. A solution to this remains to be found.

The European Court of Human Rights recently gave a decision in a case where a criminal had committed a serious crime in Italy and was illegally extradited from France via Switzerland to Italy.[3] He received substantial financial compensation from the Court in Strasbourg because his human right was violated by the illegality of the extradition.[4] Is that justified or is that going too far? Whatever your answer is to this question, it must be clear that in an integrated Europe extradition should be facilitated.

Notes and references

This paper was delivered as a lecture in April 1988 at which time the author was holder of the Leverhulme Chair at Queen Mary College under their co-operation agreement with Leiden University.
1. Judgment of 9 October 1979, Series A, No. 32.
2. After the delivery of this lecture, the European Commission of Human Rights concluded that a conviction solely based on testimonies of anonymous witnesses is contrary to Article 6: Kostovski Case of 12 May 1988.
3. Judgment of 18 December 1986, Series A, No. 111.
4. Judgment of 2 December 1987, Series A, No. 124 F.

7

The United Nations Human Rights Committee

ROSALYN HIGGINS

Among the United Nations bodies that deal with human rights, the Human Rights Committee is often confused with the Commission on Human Rights. The Commission is a subsidiary body of the Economic and Social Council, which is given special duties under the Charter in relationship to human rights, and it is a body of state representatives and highly politicised. It is a body in which supporting one's friends' record often assumes priority along with attacking the human rights of those who are not one's friends. The Commission has its own subsidiary body, the Sub-Commission on Minorities and on the Prevention of Discrimination which is staffed by individual experts who feel they are more impartial in their work. But it too is a fairly political body in a rather robust sense, while still putting out some very serious and worthwhile studies, including a study in progress at the moment on the right of freedom of movement which is to be an updating of Ingles' great report published some 20 years ago. The Sub-Commission does a great deal of important study work.

Informal relationship with the UN

The Human Rights Committee, on which I sit, is something different, because it is not part of the United Nations machinery at all. We are a treaty body: the Civil and Political Covenant of the United Nations is an international treaty and it is as part of the machinery of that treaty that the Committee exists. We have in fact formally no direct constitutional relationship to the United Nations – we are not obliged to report to anyone and we are not subject to direction by anyone or any body within the United Nations system. The reality is that we do prepare an annual report that we send to the General Assembly, where it is considered by the Third Committee. That is the Committee that deals with human rights and it is there that the states parties to the treaty particularly have a chance to air their views on how they think we are doing, taking any particular points of interest from the previous year. Again, we are subject to no directions and no mandates from above. The

This chapter was submitted in 1988.

other anomaly is that, although we are a treaty body, we are unlike the other treaty bodies, for example the committee that deals with the Convention against all Forms of Racial Discrimination – the CERD as it is known. Unlike some of those bodies we are not financed simply by the states parties – we are, rather curiously, financed by the United Nations membership as a whole. This is anomalous but in fact it works fairly advantageously for us. We have had cuts in the context of the United Nations' financial crisis but we have been able to have a say, as a treaty body, in how the savings are to be made and have been successful in that. The sad reality is that states at the moment are setting up numerous bodies to deal with particular aspects of human rights and then decide they have not the money for them to operate properly. That is why the new Committee under the Torture Convention had serious problems even before it had its very first meeting. We are more protected than most in terms of our independence. Our funding is spread over the whole of the United Nations and is included in the general budget, and so we are a little more protected.

Function of the Committee

Our function is to monitor the International Covenant on Civil and Political Rights. The history of there being two Covenants is well known. The original intention was that the United Nations Declaration on Human Rights should be turned into a more detailed instrument and in doing that the rights in it should be turned into binding legal obligations. That rapidly became an impossible task to achieve for a variety of reasons. Firstly, some of the rights turned out with the passage of time to be controversial. Thus the right to property in the original Universal Declaration has no part in the treaty versions of that Declaration that have come forward. Second, there were great difficulties in putting economic, social and cultural rights in the same instrument as civil and political rights. Among the reasons is the fact that the achievement of civil and political rights is within the reach of all states if they have a mind to give effect to them with goodwill and determination. There is no reason relating either to political philosophy or the stage of economic development that makes it impossible for a state today to provide freedom from torture, freedom of movement, freedom of expression, security of the person. However, with the economic and social rights it is extremely hard for many of the developing countries to provide those rights today or even, indeed, tomorrow. The timetable for the implementation of economic and social rights is more flexible and it was felt that the implementation machinery should be less rigorous.

Consequently two Covenants came into being and it is the Covenant on Civil and Political Rights that has the more effective machinery. From the outset it was envisaged that there would be a Committee that would assist in the implementation of rights under that Covenant. That was not the original intention under the Economic Social and Cultural Covenant. That Covenant did have a reporting system built into it but the reports were to go straight to the Economic and Social Council – a United Nations political body – and it was an altogether softer and more politicised system of monitoring. In fact it has now been agreed by the states parties to that other Covenant that they too should have a committee and this has recently come into existence. It does only some of the things we do and does not have the possibility of individual cases being brought before it. But there has now been established an independent body of experts not part of the regular United Nations political machinery to receive states reports. Those reports are more frequent than ours and shorter; less detailed but none the less a step along the right road. But the Civil and Political Covenant for the moment has weightier monitoring machinery.

Let me just make this point in passing about the rights we speak of: the Civil and Political Covenant contains the core civil and political rights. It is divided into parts and interestingly there stands in Part 1 all alone in one Article the right to self-determination and within that idea the free disposition of one's own natural resources. That right is clearly of a different order and nature from all the other rights which are individual rights. Even minority rights are cast that way. In Part 2 of the Covenant one has certain preliminary matters dealt with, to which I will return. In Part 3 one has the rest of the substantive rights. These are the sort of rights you would expect in such an instrument: right to life, freedom from torture, freedom from slavery and servitude, impermissibility of imprisonment for failure to meet a contractual obligation, freedom of movement, equality, fair trial provision, non-retrospection in penal matters, privacy, freedom of thought, religion, conscience, expression and assembly, and certain other Articles are also there.

Some of these Articles may not be derogated from. Part 2 allows some derogation in limited circumstances in times of national emergency. There is a wide list of rights under the Covenant that may not be derogated from that is wider than the comparable list under the European Convention on Human Rights. Some of the rights that we have do not appear at all under the European Convention. For example, in Article 13 there is a special clause on the rights of aliens to which we make frequent reference. In Article 10 there is a special clause about the treatment of persons lawfully deprived of their liberty. There is an Article which prohibits propaganda against war, and an Article relating to family life and the rights of the child. In Article 26 there is equality before the law, and non-discrimination in that regard different from general non-discrimination. There is also a separate Article on minorities (Article 27).

Part 4 of the Covenant deals with the machinery, and it is Article 28 of the Covenant that provides that there shall be a Human Rights Committee to consist of 18 members from different parts of the world. There is an unofficial understanding that the distribution of membership should reflect the geographic distribution of ratifying states parties. It is a fact that for the moment Asia is rather undersubscribed – the Asian states parties to the Covenant are not proportionally as high as South American, Eastern European and Western European. The Committee has three main functions, one of which is in respect of particular provisions for interstate disputes on human rights. Article 41 does allow for states to make a special declaration that they will recognise the competence of the Committee to deal with applications in which one state party claims that another state party is violating the human rights under this instrument. That provision is in effect and one might have expected that in a diverse system, where parties come from different regions and do not have the like-mindedness that one sees under the European Convention, there would be a flood of such claims from states hostile to each other. But the Committee has yet to have any work at all under that heading.

As to our other functions, the first relates to the state reports, provided for under Article 40 of the Civil and Political Covenant. Article 40 provides that the states parties undertake to submit reports on the measures they have adopted to give effect to the rights, and progress they are making in the enjoyment of those rights. Article 40 also provides that they must submit the report within one year of the entry into force of the Covenant for them and thereafter whenever the Committee so requests. What has happened is this: the Committee does expect initial reports to come within one year of ratification; then a decision was taken – 'the decision on periodicity' – by which we call in subsequent reports every five years. Five years seems a substantial period to elapse but one needs to appreciate the extreme thoroughness of the investigative process. My view is that if that reporting system were to happen more frequently, as with other instruments, there would not be the same calibre of examination regarding each state that we now have.

Reporting procedure

Concerning the question of initial reports legally required to come within a year, for the large part they have completed and delivered. A few states have yet to submit theirs but some are those whose general image in human rights is not the best. The initial report examination is done in the following way: each member of the Committee having done his or her research in advance on the report that comes in (translated into all the working languages) is then able to ask whatever questions he or she wishes of the state representatives who are present for an examination on that report. So each member of the

Committee may take 20 minutes putting his range of concerns and will then expect to have answers there and then. We term this 'a constructive dialogue'. We are not there merely to criticise a country or give it marks out of ten, and we try to communicate that at the beginning of the process and then engage in this quite informal exchange. We are now up to most of the second periodic reports, and indeed the third periodic reports for early ratifying countries are also coming in. Here we have a quite different technique that has emerged through practice, and it is nowhere to be found in rules of procedure. By a second report the Committee ought to be able to go into depth on what is happening in a particular country. By that stage we have a much better understanding of the legal system and realities of that country. So the Committee have issued what are called 'guidelines' which tell the states how we would like those reports to be handled. We ask them to go through every single Article of the Covenant and tell us not only about the laws in their country in relation to each but the administrative practices, the political realities and the problems. We encourage the sharing of problems and difficulties with us. Before a specific periodic report examination, a working group will suggest a list of issues that the state should be prepared to deal with under each of the Articles. The working group will have picked up particular things from the state report. That proposal gets attended to on the very first day by the plenary Committee and as soon as the list of specific questions is agreed it goes straight away over to the mission of the country concerned. It tells the government that we would like the discussion to be clustered in a particular way and we ask for answers to be prepared to the set list of questions. During that dialogue matters will proceed issue by issue with as many members who wish speaking on each particular issue, rather than one member trying to go through everything. It is a much more rigorous method and we find that periodic reports take about five sessions, which is a very considerable period of time. We on the Committee are aware of the problems both for us and the states. For us we have a lot of reports to get through and this sometimes means we have to keep states waiting after they put reports in, maybe a few months. From the point of view of the states of course it means a great deal of preparation both in terms of a long and detailed report and allowing their senior civil servants time with us when they have other pressing duties. We try in a three-week session to deal with four reports; indeed, since 1988 we have sometimes dealt with five, and even six.

Case law

In addition to the state reporting mechanism there is also the case law under the Covenant. The case law, referred to as 'communications' rather than 'applications', arises out of a separate Protocol to the Covenant. States may become ratifying parties to an Optional Protocol to the Covenant, thus allowing individuals to bring complaints against them concerning human rights violations within their jurisdiction. The human rights must of course be those human rights that are to be found in the Covenant. There is an anomaly that that has led to. Self-determination is a group collective right that exists in a separate part of the Covenant and we have had recently to face the problem of whether an individual can under the Protocol bring a complaint regarding self-determination, which is not an individual right. After very extended deliberations we found that they cannot. For the moment there does not seem to be the possibility of action under the Protocol in respect of self-determination.

A typical case comes to the Committee in the following way. An individual writes complaining of a violation of his rights and this might be addressed to us or to the United Nations. It does not matter how informal it is; it will get looked at and if it appears to relate to the Covenant it will be directed to the Committee. A working group meets for a week before the three-week session to take an initial look at a new case. We will be looking to see, first of all, that the complaint is made by the victim or someone that can stand in the shoes of the victim such as the next of kin or the victim's lawyer. One cannot make complaints in the abstract. Secondly, we will be looking to see it is at least arguable that it relates to a right under the Covenant. We look also to see if it is absolutely clear that local remedies have been exhausted, because it is a requirement of our Covenant, as it is of every human rights treaty, that these matters be dealt with at the local level first. At that stage it is possible, once the communication gets past those very initial hurdles, to send the dossier off to the state concerned under a 'rule 91' decision. It goes off to the state concerned seeking information and explanations, whether local remedies have in fact been exhausted, whether our initial understandings are correct, and also for any initial comments about the admissibility of that case before us.

The state is required to reply within a certain time and if the state fails to meet the deadline that will work to its disadvantage, in the sense that we will then take as a working premise the facts asserted by the victim. It is an extremely useful technique to encourage a non-assisting state actually to participate and meet the time limits it is required to under the treaty. The Committee then examines the dossier anew to take an admissibility decision, and this requires at this stage looking in much more considerable depth. We do a final check that the case is not being dealt with elsewhere, a situation that occasionally comes up in the context of the European Convention, and more frequently for us in the context of the Inter-American Convention. We cannot take on a case that is being dealt with by another body. We will look to see whether there are any reservations by the state that make it impossible for us to proceed further. The admissibility decisions can often be very complex and difficult.

For persons wanting to follow these matters, there are two volumes of collected decisions to date. The non-admissibility decisions stand alone and the admissibility decisions are found as part and parcel of the decision on the merits. Once a case has got over the admissibility hurdle, both parties are then asked to make further observations on the merits. When these are finally received we are then in a position to make a decision on the merits which we call our 'Views'. The cases cover a variety of issues ranging from what we could call technical violations of human rights (but none the less extremely real for the individual) to the grosser forms of violations of human rights that one sees much more rarely under the European Convention system where one is dealing with more like-minded democracies. Cases of torture, disappearances, summary executions, are received not as a broad administrative practice but as a complaint by an individual, a person's family or his lawyer. Also we get the technical cases where perhaps there is more opportunity for refinement of the law; developing one's jurisprudence with a rather more subtle brush. The Committee's practice on local remedies is extremely similar to that of the European Convention. We have had the same problem, for example if a lawyer has advised that a case can go no further. We too have had to determine what happens if the state is not providing adequate remedies itself. Does that allow one not to have to exhaust even fruitless remedies? All of those matters concerning local remedies arising under the European Convention are to be found in our jurisprudence too.

There are particular problems about successor governments. In the last few years we have witnessed the phenomenon where in many countries and in particular Latin America there has been a move back to democracy. We have cases still coming through relating to such countries as Uruguay concerning grave violations that were carried out under the previous military regime, and we have had difficult decisions to take about how to handle those. We have taken the view that it is the *state* that is party, and that therefore insofar as there are adverse findings to be made, they are against Uruguay (and not against the present democratic government). We hope that the phraseology that we introduce is clear to the present government with its very welcome return to democracy and collaboration with our committee.

Finally, some interesting recent topics have arisen in the case law. We have recently had to deal with an issue that the European Convention had to deal with some time back, namely protection in administrative suits. We have a clause that is comparable to Article 6 of the European Convention, but which is not identical, and we have needed to decide whether all administrative decisions need some type of judicial review. We have not been helped by the fact that there are discrepancies in the language versions of the Covenant nor by the fact that certain members of the Committee feel that the uncertain road down which the European Convention organs have gone on Article 6 is a good reason for shutting the door early. But we have kept the door open and I welcome that. The path we will tread will not necessarily be the same as that taken in Europe.

Another extremely important area has been under Article 26, with its 'equal protection of the law' clause. We have had to decide whether that clause (which stands quite separately from the requirement of non-discrimination in respect of Covenant rights) means that if we find a discriminatory practice in relation to a right that is *not* in our Covenant, we have jurisdiction over it. For example, pension rights are not guaranteed in our Covenant. But if pensions are provided in a discriminatory fashion, does Article 26 both allow and require us to deal with that case? This was an extremely difficult decision which we answered in the summer of 1987 in the affirmative. We have held that if benefits are granted by law or burdens imposed by law, it must be done without discrimination. At the same time, not every difference is discriminatory. It will depend upon whether it is justified by its purpose and objective need.

8

Human rights and legal services

WALTER MERRICKS

Few of those who have attempted to draft international conventions on human rights have expressly referred to the availability of legal services. This is perhaps hardly surprising. It is not a basic human right to have access at all times to a lawyer, let alone to the unlimited services of a lawyer paid at public expense. Moreover it would be a sad world in which legal services were so indispensable that access to them became described as a human right. Most of us would prefer to live our lives without having to deal with lawyers, and the need to consult a lawyer is rightly seen by most people as a necessary evil and a last resort.

This exposition does not lead to the conclusion that there is nothing further to be said on the subject of human rights and legal services. There are areas where access to a lawyer is a human right. Access to the law itself can also be seen as an essential provision. Just as the independence of the courts may be an essential pre-condition for the exercise of one's ordinary rights, so also is the existence of an independent legal profession. Finally, human rights law needs human rights lawyers; not just academic lawyers refining and distinguishing lines of case law, but lawyers conversant with human rights law and willing and able to advise clients on the means of enforcement.

The one area in which the right to a lawyer is singled out for mention in most of the international covenants on human rights is that of criminal defence. For instance, Article 6 of the European Convention on Human Rights states that everyone charged with a criminal offence has the right to defend himself in person or through legal assistance of his own choosing or, if he has not sufficient means to pay for legal assistance, to be given it free when the interests of justice so require. Similar provisions are to be found in the United Nations International Covenant on Civil and Political Rights. Clearly the person accused of a criminal offence is having the weight of the state's resources thrown against him or her and stands in danger of substantial penalties including the loss of liberty. Criminal courts are courts of law and the accused person needs advice from an expert in the law to know even whether he has indeed committed the offence with which he has been charged. The accused should be given the chance to protect his own interests and must therefore be afforded someone to advise and counsel him

---

This chapter was submitted in 1987.

in an unfamiliar system what his best interests are and how they are best served. I think, however, that the right to a criminal defence lawyer is more important in systems where the law itself is complex, and also where the state devotes substantial legal resources in the form of legally qualified prosecutors to establishing the case against the accused. One can for instance envisage a state in which accusations of crime are preferred by officials who are not lawyers, before judges who have no legal training, and where the criminal laws of the state consist of very general prohibitions. (I could here of course be describing the procedure in an English magistrates' court up until the advent of the Crown Prosecution Service). In such systems justice may not require that the accused be provided with the services of a lawyer. The requirement of access to a lawyer is therefore partly a balancing provision ensuring a more equal provision of legal services between the prosecution and the defence. In adversarial systems of law this equality of provision is of even greater importance than in inquisitorial systems where the court itself plays a key role in pursuing the inquiry.

Choice of lawyer

Both the two international human rights treaties to which I have referred emphasise that the accused shall have the right to a lawyer of his own choosing. The lawyer should not simply be assigned to him regardless of his wishes. He must be able to satisfy himself that the lawyer is an independent lawyer, not a state employee or a full-time prosecutor who will not act in his best interests.

The more important obligation imposed on states by Article 6 is that legal assistance should be given free when the interests of justice so require to persons who have insufficient means to pay for it. Naturally this begs the question of whether justice does so require it in any particular case, but clearly a system in which no one ever had access to free legal assistance would be unlikely to comply with the convention.

It is perhaps interesting to examine the system of criminal legal aid in England and Wales. Legal assistance is given by private practising solicitors and barristers and over 90 per cent of those appearing in the Crown Court receive legal aid. Criminal legal aid is a means-tested service and applicants are often asked to contribute financially to the cost of the service they receive. However, unless the accused obviously has the resources to pay for his own legal representation, legal aid is virtually never refused. Although applicants are entitled to express preferences about the lawyer they wish to represent them, there is no legal right under the criminal legal aid scheme to choose one's own solicitor or barrister. The position is formally that the court assigns to the accused person a solicitor - normally the one he has chosen. There are, however, circumstances in which the accused will be assigned a solicitor against his wishes. The most frequent case in which this occurs is where persons are jointly charged. The practice of the courts is to assign the same solicitor to act for all those on a joint charge on the grounds that separate representation would be excessively expensive and unnecessary. The second situation occurs where an accused person has lost confidence in the solicitor he first chose and wishes to change solicitors. Permission for this is sometimes granted but sometimes refused – particularly where one change has already taken place – again on the ground of expense.

As far as the right to choose one's barrister is concerned, this is often in practice honoured, but just as often is not. The Crown Court listing system and the number of barristers available in practice are such that in a substantial minority of cases the accused winds up with a barrister who was not the barrister that he and his solicitor chose. The Crown Court listing system can often mean that cases are called on at very short notice – sometimes even the defence lawyers will be informed at 4 o'clock the day before. In such circumstances it is often inevitable that the barrister originally selected is not available. It is the function of the Crown Court of the listing officer to decide whether or not the non-availability of the defendant's barrister should be regarded as a sufficient ground for not listing the case the following day. Rarely do they accept that as a sufficient ground; nor probably could they if the system is not to grind to a halt. The aphorism often used here is that a defendant has a right to counsel of his own choice – but not necessarily of his first choice. The choice of barristers available at 4 o'clock in the afternoon who are free the following day is of necessity fairly limited. There is unfortunately little accurate information, either nationally or by way of research samples, showing the number of defendants who had appeared at the Crown Court represented by barristers who were not their original first choice (or more accurately, not the first choice of their solicitor). It is this restriction on the choice of representative which must be one of the strongest arguments for permitting solicitors rights of audience in the Crown Court.

The question of whether within the context of the British system a public defender service – that is a service employing salaried lawyers to carry out defence work – has often been discussed. Recently both the Law Society and the Bar took proceedings against the Lord Chancellor over the rates of remuneration offered to lawyers undertaking criminal legal aid defence work. It was said at that time that unless the rates were substantially increased there was a danger that the work would become uneconomic for private practitioners to continue. Since that time the government has published an 'Efficiency Scrutiny' on the legal aid scheme. While that does not go so far as to propose a public defender service, it discusses the employment of salaried solicitors to carry out civil legal aid work. Clearly the day might come when the Treasury found it an attractive option to see the establishment of a career defence service where there could be tighter control over the salary structure, the hours worked and the total costs of the scheme. Although there are some lawyers who would not be averse to the establishment of such a service, the right of the defendant to choose his lawyer and to choose a genuinely independent lawyer must be preserved. I would certainly hope that in any such system the right of the defendant to choose an independent lawyer in private practice would still at least be preserved. This would serve to ensure that the standard of service provided by the state defender service was at least as attractive to accused persons as those provided elsewhere.

Access to the law

I now turn to a subject which has not traditionally been identified within codified conventions as a human right but is in my view an important and fundamental obligation of the state. Surprisingly it has been the subject of little concern among lawyers or other commentators. This could be defined as the state's obligation to ensure that its laws are available in an understandable fashion to lay people. The proposition may appear self-evident, yet very little attention has been given to accomplishing this objective. Over the past twenty years much has been accomplished through our legal aid scheme to make courts accessible. Perhaps in future the emphasis should also be placed on making law accessible. Not only is it in the interests of the layman to have access to the law, but the legal system itself benefits from informed comment by the layman, comment which obviously cannot be informed without some knowledge of the law.

Lay people acquire their knowledge of the law from a number of sources. These are wide and varied sources and include of course lawyers themselves, statutes, textbooks on the law, consumers' rights guides, official leaflets, and radio and television programmes both of a fictional and non-fictional kind. As far as the substantive statutory law is concerned the Law Commission has undertaken the major task of codifying English law – a task which will clearly not be completed even by the end of the century. Even if it is completed, it is clear that the English technique for legal drafting of statutes would mean that the resulting code or codes would not be easy reading. Their attempts at codification are not necessarily designed for the lay person and the lay person who seriously wants to understand what the law is on a certain subject currently has to choose between *Halsbury's Laws of England* and the *Reader's Digest Guide to the Law*. Commercial publishers not unnaturally do not see the production of an encyclopaedia of law for non-lawyers as being an important or attractive proposition. The only non-commercial publication which attempts to meet this need is the excellently produced *Citizens Advice Notes*, which is produced as an aid to Citizens Advice Bureaux workers but is not directly available to the public. It is interesting to note that over ten years ago the Law Reform Commission of Canada recommended the production of an encyclopaedia of law for non-lawyers and set out in some detail how the encyclopaedia should be constructed, written and produced. So far as I know no action has yet been taken to implement the Commission's proposals, but I suspect that before long this country and others will come under increasing pressure to make the law more accessible to the citizen. I think that the citizen is entitled without payment to reasonably comprehensible statements of the law which is liable to affect him or her. An increasing emphasis on this might be a salutory experience for lawyers, law-makers and academic commentators.

Independence of the legal profession

A further threat to access to legal services, although perhaps a rather distant and long-term one, concerns the independence of the legal profession in the following way. Solicitors and barristers have always accepted restrictions on the methods in which they can practise in order to preserve their independence. Barristers cannot be employed by anyone, nor can they employ another barrister or be in partnership with another barrister. Solicitors are permitted to employ other solicitors, but are not presently permitted to be employed by persons other than solicitors. Solicitors and indeed barristers may be employed by a lay employer solely for the purpose of giving advice to that employer but not being held out as practising publicly. Many such lawyers practise within commerce, industry and government both central and local.

What is now proposed, however, is that commercial institutions should be able to employ solicitors to provide legal services (conveyancing) for the general public. This proposal arises from the Building Societies Act 1986 which permits commercial institutions to provide conveyancing services. This issue stands wholly apart from the question of whether lending bodies would have a conflict of interest should they provide conveyancing services for borrowers. Once the non-employment principle has been breached it would be difficult to resist the idea that solicitors could be employed by other commercial institutions to provide all legal services. There are two views one can take about such potential developments. One school of thought holds that independence is an attitude of mind automatically developed by lawyers and could withstand being subjected to employment by commercial institutions. After all, if the lawyers' code of professional conduct is worth anything it is strong enough to survive operating from within a commercial context. The other school argues that professional standards and the independence of advice spring only from a carefully nurtured tradition of independent practice. This could be crushed by the corporatism of the large institutions, profit targets, work-flow formulae, the promotion hierarchy and such like.

Would it really be desirable to see firms of solicitors swallowed up by commercial institutions? With the sale over the last year of large numbers of estate agents' firms to insurance companies, building societies and banks, the idea can hardly be regarded as fanciful. In the present climate in the City of London, dual or multiple capacity seems to be the order of the day. No doubt it would be attractive to the big firms of accountants, and the big City conglomerates, to join forces with law firms. Building societies, instead of employing solicitors, might find it easier simply to buy existing practices. All the big City firms might in due course become part of large financial conglomerates, while the more successful provincial practices would become wholly owned subsidiaries of banks, building societies or insurance companies. Independent practitioners trying to start up in practice and looking for overdrafts might find banks prepared to loan funds only in return for an equity stake and a veto on unprofitable (legal aid) work.

Beyond the conveyancing field it is clear that the Legal Aid Scrutiny had in mind a major expansion in the salaried sector. Law centre lawyers (of whom I was one) would all argue that their independence is not compromised by being employed by a lay body. Law centres are rightly insulated from their paymasters by a lay management committee which is able to protect the solicitors from any pressure to compromise their professional standards. One could not be so sure if the government took a more controlling influence in the development of the salaried sector. The penny-pinching way it has gone about establishing the Crown Prosecution Service is no encouragement. (At least the CPS acts only for the Crown – a similarly funded public defender system would not be good news for those who were its clients.)

Although this threat to the independence of the legal profession is far distant and arises in the context of a service (conveyancing) which many clearly now no longer regard as a professional legal service, it should be taken seriously since the breach of principle involved is a fundamental one, and there is no easy point at which a halt could be called.

Here then are three strands of different aspects of current legal services policy, which I have attempted to indicate have the hallmarks of fundamental, essential or human rights.

9

Patients, doctors and human rights

IAN KENNEDY

Introduction

My concern is with what I will call medical law. The question for consideration is whether there is anything to be gained analytically or practically in approaching medical law in terms of human rights. I will suggest that there is and that a number of recent developments in medical law should properly be seen as involving issues of human rights. I will argue further that if they had been seen in this way, they might well have been analysed and even decided differently.

As a medical lawyer my first task, of course, may be to persuade the doubters – and there are many – that there is a field which can properly be designated medical law. There are still those who regard the law relating to medical practice as merely involving the application of the general law of torts, or criminal law, or family law, or whatever, to the particular facts. To continue to adopt this view is to lose sight of at least two important considerations. The first is that there are certain themes of an ethical nature which run through and underlie medical practice and which must be taken account of in any legal analysis. By contrast, if medical practice is dealt with in an *ad hoc* way, this fact may well be overlooked. A consequence could be (and has been in the past) that legal developments in relation to medical practice lack the kind of internal coherence and consistency of principle which an understanding of the underlying themes would produce. This objection, I may say, is not made out of concern for logical niceties. Rather, it is to say that the law is the poorer and that the interests of patients, doctors and the community are less well served if such a state of affairs prevails.

Human rights

Secondly, an approach to the law regulating the practice of medicine which treats it as if it were just another application of the law of battery, or negligence, or child custody, seriously neglects a dimension which can broadly be called human rights. It neglects the need to take account of certain broad over-arching legal *as well as* ethical principles against which any proposed

This chapter was submitted in 1990.

legal measure must be tested and approved. And, when I talk of human rights here, I would make it clear that I refer not only to those rights declared in international Conventions or set down in the Constitutions or Charters of particular nations, but also those inchoate rights which are the product of reasoned moral analysis.

It is fair to say, however, that talk of rights or human rights in the context of medical law has often provoked a hostile reaction from those who claim to speak for the medical profession. This is because the rights discussed are asserted as the rights of patients. Such assertions do not sit well with a profession which is, quite properly, educated to think of itself as concerned with the difficult task of caring for the sick and seeking to overcome illness. Talk of rights is often represented to the doctor as if it inevitably involves confrontation, legalism and strict or rigid restrictions on what the doctor may do. A further impression exists that reference to rights often provokes litigation, with the regrettable consequence of what has come to be known as 'defensive medicine'. Thus, some say, it is far better to avoid such talk of rights. Better to talk in terms of trust, it is said, and let doctors get on with their job.

The weakness of these counter-arguments does not need exposure here. But despite their lack of substance they survive with great tenacity. Trust, for example, has to be earned and is not the birthright of the doctor or any other professional. Equally, the history of mankind, and even of doctors, is that some sort of social system for overseeing the activities of those who enjoy privileges as regards others is appropriate, indeed is essential. Any such system must inevitably consist of principles and rules guiding conduct. It may, of course, be a system of self-regulation, whereby the profession governs itself. Few, however, would now maintain that this is enough and, of course, to do so is somewhat forlorn since the existence of legal regulation of, for example, medicine is a social fact. Further, it must never be assumed that it is only the doctor who is concerned for the interests of the patient, while the lawyer is some interfering wrecker. The lawyer is equally concerned with the patient's interests, is concerned indeed with the patient's human rights. That the two professions may disagree on how these rights should best be protected in any particular case does not entail that the lawyer is necessarily wrong, far less interfering.

However, even when the existence of and perhaps the need for law is granted, there is still the tendency to state and analyse the law wholly in terms of duties, the duties of doctors and perhaps of patients, so as to avoid what is perceived (wrongly) as the more oppressive language of rights. For, to adopt the language of rights – of patients' rights – is, it is argued, to restrict the freedom to practice, the so-called clinical freedom of the doctor. That any assertion of clinical freedom is as much an appeal to rights – the rights of doctors – is sometimes lost on its proponents. And, of course, to argue that patients have rights is not necessarily to deprive doctors of discretion. Rather, it aims to set the framework within which such discretion may properly be exercised.

So, I will adopt here a frank assertion of rights inherent in the doctor – patient relationship. Apart from arguments of principle which elaborate the basis and nature of such rights, I assert them for a further contingent reason. As between the doctor and the patient there is an inevitable imbalance or disequilibrium of power. The doctor has information and skill which the patient, who lacks these, wishes to employ for his benefit. When it is remembered that among the powers possessed by the doctor is the privilege to touch and even invade the body of another and as a consequence exercise control to a greater or lesser extent over that person, it will be clear that, with the best will in the world, and conceding the good faith of the doctors, such powers must be subject to control and scrutiny, from an abundance of caution. This is the role of patients' rights, whereby the permissible limits are set by ethics and law to the exercise of the doctor's power.

Perhaps I should make it clear, before proceeding further, that as a matter of ethical analysis, when I talk of rights in the context of medical practice, I am talking of prima facie rights rather than absolute rights. This is not to deny that absolute rights may be urged by some. Instead, it is to suggest that in the everyday practice of medicine by civilised doctors in a civilised community, such absolute rights, if they exist, are not usually called into play. Thus, the rights we are concerned with are prima facie to be observed, by which I mean that they are to be observed in the absence of any powerful justifying argument which allows them to be overridden. And, of course, any such justification must itself be derived from a morally sound principle.

As a further clarification, I should draw attention to the distinction often made as a matter of law between human rights and civil rights.[1] On this analysis, human rights are those rights recognised by international law, while civil rights are those which translate human rights into the law of particular states. I will use the general term 'human rights' throughout, leaving the context to indicate which meaning is appropriate. To complete the introduction to human rights in the context of medical practice and finally to dispel the doubts of the disbeliever, I should point to their recognition both on an international plane and in other countries similar in most respects to our own. I need only mention, for example, the Nuremburg Code followed by the Declaration of Helsinki[2] concerning the rights of those who may be the subject of medical research. In the United States, the Constitution has been prayed in aid to guarantee, for example, access to contraception by virtue of the right to privacy under the 9th Amendment[3] and access to abortion, at least in the initial stages of pregnancy by virtue of the equal protection clause of the 14th Amendment.[4] In Canada, too, the Charter of Rights and Freedoms has already seen service in regulating such issues as parents objecting to the treatment of their children on religious grounds, the detention of the mentally ill and the sterilisation of the incompetent.[5] Nearer to home, we have, of course, the European Convention on Human Rights, a number of Articles of which have been used to assert the rights of patients.[6]

Examples

So much for introduction. Let me now give you some examples of circumstances of medical practice in which it must be clear that considerations of human rights are involved. In terms of factual circumstances the examples come tumbling over themselves. They include – and I make no judgments here but merely recite examples – the compulsory detention of the mentally ill and the compulsory treatment of them; research on humans, treatment at the end of life which may mean that death arrives sooner rather than later (sometimes referred to as euthanasia in its various forms); the care of the newborn baby and what is perhaps euphemistically called selective non-treatment; contraception; abortion; research on embryos; transsexualism; and the huge issue of resource allocation and access to care. These problems touch on such rights as the right to life, the right to privacy, the right to marry and found a family, the right to the opportunity to reproduce, the right to be free from inhuman treatment and the right to free movement. As I have indicated, they are, by and large, prima facie rights, such that, for example, compulsory treatment or detention may be justified and may not therefore be a violation of human rights if good, morally sound reasons can be given for imposing them.

English law's response

Consent

All of these issues have attracted the attention of English law, whether by legislation or judicial decision; the response of English law has been to consider them as *ad hoc* factual problems to be dealt with by reference to traditional legal frameworks. As I have suggested, however, this may not be satisfactory. It may well cause certain themes and principles to be lost sight of. For example, it is clear that the single most important theme which runs through the examples I have given is the theme of *consent*. And consent is, of course, the legal and ethical expression of the human right to respect for autonomy and self-determination. Lawyers who fail to recognise this and other such unifying themes may find themselves fighting the cause of patients on difficult ground, where everything turns on the meaning of a sub-clause of a statute, and in circumstances in which the court has been mesmerised once again by the spectre of doom which would follow any holding of liability against the doctor. Lawyers who do recognise the central role of human rights argue their cases against a wider background and take their cases further, out of the narrow confines of domestic law and into the more understanding environment of, for example, the European Convention on Human Rights. No one better epitomised this approach than Larry Gostin when Legal Director of MIND (the National Association for Mental Health). Perhaps it was his training in the United States which made him think in terms of an appeal to human rights.[7] In any event, his resort to the European Convention created a minor revolution in mental health law. Perhaps the only English judge who shares this understanding is Lord Scarman, a committed advocate of human rights. His speech in the leading case of *Sidaway* v. *Bethlem Royal Hospital Governors*,[8] for example, made it clear that, when considering the issue of informed consent, he at least could see beyond the narrow issue of who said what, and what doctors thought was good practice, to the fact that when we consider the duty of the doctor to inform his patients we are concerned with a profoundly important human right: the right to control one's own destiny by knowing what it is that will be done by way of treatment, so that one may say no, if so minded.

Seeing and understanding the legal concept of consent as the expression of the right to autonomy provides us with an ever-present example of, and alerts us to the need to recognise and explore, this unifying ethical theme or principle when considering apparently disparate areas of medical practice. First, respect for autonomy, in the form of a requirement of consent before a person may be touched, is contingent on the competence of the person to consent. Autonomy is not respected if reliance is placed on the expression of view of an incompetent person. The treatment of the mentally ill, the mentally handicapped, the senile, or the child, while medically different, each have this in common and prompt a search at the level of abstract analysis for an appropriate meaning of competence and ways of establishing it. Secondly, respect for autonomy translated as the legal requirement of consent must also take account of whether the consent is given voluntarily. Out of this grows the notion of vulnerability. It becomes clear that it is not only a violation of respect for autonomy to *compel* someone to be treated, but also to take advantage of, or prey on, the vulnerability of patients to gain apparent consent. In this way, such different questions as whether it is right to treat compulsorily the mentally ill or the pregnant woman who refuses a Caesarean section, to offer relief from prison on terms that the sex offender undergo castrating hormone therapy, or to take advantage of the prisoner, the impecunious unemployed or the patient-anxious-to-please by enrolling them as 'volunteers' in research, are seen as variations on a common theme. Finally, respect for autonomy in the legal form of consent requires an examination of whether the consent is appropriately informed. The whole range of interchanges between doctor and patient, from simple injection or prescription of medicine to life-saving operations, fall to be analysed by reference to this central principle as law and ethics seek to respond to the disequilibrium of power between doctor and patient.

Sidaway

This mention of the need for consent to be informed if it is to be regarded as valid takes us back to the case of *Sidaway* which I referred to earlier. As is now well known, the case concerned a claim by Mrs Sidaway that had she known of the risks associated with the proposed surgery to relieve pain in her neck, she would never have consented to it. The House of Lords dismissed her case. It was impossible, they said, to know precisely what had passed between her and her now dead surgeon. But the House of Lords did take the opportunity to comment at length on the law of consent.[9] As I have said, it was only Lord Scarman who saw the case in the wider context of human rights. The implications of the case were not, however, lost on the other members of the House of Lords. All realised it was a landmark decision: a challenge to the conservatism of the medical profession and its continuing validation via the courts. All realised that their analysis of the law could be couched in terms of patients' rights or doctors' duties. All but Lord Scarman chose, with more or less enthusiasm, the traditional analytical model of English law, that of duties. They preferred the safer and more limited ground of doctors' duties. In this way they could at the same time tinker with the scope of a doctor's responsibility to his patient while expressing it in terms of its being a concession to the patient, arising out of a proper understanding of the doctor's duty rather than a legitimate right flowing from the patient's civic status as a person entitled to control what is done to him by others, even if done in the name of treatment.

The language of patients' rights was lost in the rhetoric of imminent doom which, if those who claimed to speak for the medical profession were to be believed, would follow any weakening of the doctor's control over the doctor – patient relationship. If not quite arguing that lions would whelp in the streets, it would, we were all assured, be a *bad day for medicine*, and with the grand sweep of those unembarrassed by paternalism, for patients. Introduce the right of a patient to be informed, (albeit with carefully crafted provisos) and the excesses of US style litigation (largely imagined) would follow as night follows day.[10] Why doctors should be in a special position goes unanalysed. That the doctor's client is a patient is thought to be sufficient argument. Why being a patient should *ipso facto* weaken a person's claim to have his rights respected goes unanswered. Imagine a solicitor instructed to handle the sale of a house by a client. Imagine then that the solicitor, without informing the client, accepts on the client's behalf a price well below the reserve specified by the client, or purports to sell the contents of the house at the same time. Imagine then that when challenged by the client the solicitor responds that he thought it wrong to consult the client because the client was clearly distraught at the thought of the sale (occasioned, let us imagine, by the death of her spouse) and was in no condition to make a considered judgment. Imagine that the solicitor went on to say that it was indeed his duty to protect the client from such hard decisions in times of distress. Imagine then what a court would do!

Is the patient such as Mrs Sidaway, contemplating elective surgery, i.e. surgery she could take or leave, in any different position? Yes, say the courts. She is a patient. There are different rules for doctors. You may join me in wondering what I have missed in the argument! And the response is all the more regrettable because those who argue for the recognition of the rights of patients are the first to concede that the rights of the patient are only prima facie rights. If the patient really will be terrorised by being told certain things, or is too sick to take in information, it is readily recognised that true respect of the patient's rights may in such circumstances require that he is not informed. Yet still, any expression of the law in terms of patients' rights is vehemently opposed.

The only conclusion has to be that what is being rejected is not the analytical model of rights, but what recourse to the language of rights has traditionally been thought to represent. Rights are subversive. Historically, those who enjoy (in all senses of the term) power have insisted on the language of duty to express the relationship between the powerful and the rest. The assertion of rights, enjoyed by all, is by that token supremely threatening. And, what has been true historically on a grand scale, is no less true on the smaller stage of medical politics. Recognise that a patient has rights and the days of the hard-won power of the medical profession are numbered. Judges lend a sympathetic ear. After all, is it not the role of one professional elite to protect another?

As if to prove this hypothesis, the first case to apply the decision in *Sidaway* did so in a way which can only be described as deeply disappointing if not perverse. The Court of Appeal in *Gold* v. *Haringey Health Authority*[11] chose to rely on the speech in *Sidaway*, that of Lord Diplock, which had clung most tenaciously to the old 'doctor knows best' approach. It was as if the glosses put on this aphorism, albeit tentatively, by Lords Bridge and Templeman had not happened. Their speeches were certainly not mentioned. Needless to say neither was that of Lord Scarman.

The picture in this particular corner of medical law, is, therefore, rather gloomy. It will have to change. The *Bolam* principle, which (you will recall) has it that 'a doctor is not guilty of negligence if he has acted in accordance with a practice accepted as proper by a responsible body of medical men skilled in that particular art', may have some justification in matters of technical skill,[12] but its application to the question of informing (and thereby empowering) a patient is palpably indefensible.[13] It is quite beyond my comprehension how it can still be regarded as relevant to the law in this most important area of human rights.

Non-consensual sterilisation - the great challenge

If the 1980s began in Britain with virtually no developed medical law, and consequently no recognition in medical law of human rights, they certainly did not end that way. *Sidaway* in 1985 represented a major development, a major opportunity (an opportunity lost, many would say). The years 1987 and 1989 provided two cases which proved undoubtedly to be the most significant test as yet of the law's commitment to human rights in the context of medical practice. I refer to *Re B*[14] and *Re F*[15] in which the issue for the courts was, put simply, under what circumstances, if any, is it lawful to sterilise a woman without her consent?

Much has already been written about these cases,[16] and I do not intend any lengthy analysis of their place in medical law. My only concern is what they teach us about the prominence given by our highest court to considerations of human rights and the analysis such considerations should provoke.

1. Re B

I begin with the case of *Re B*. It involved the question whether it was lawful to sterilise a 17-year-old girl who was mentally handicapped and deemed incapable of giving valid consent to the proposed treatment. Here, if you will, is a classic case for an analyst of medical law. The case *could* be dealt with as if it were no more than a variant of the ordinary run of family law cases which the courts deal with every day. The girl was a minor and a ward of court. The principle that her welfare was paramount could be ritually recited and a decision taken to do that which was in her best interests.

This is how medical law cases, particularly those involving children, have routinely been treated by counsel and judges alike. In so doing, of course, the vital themes which transcend the particular facts of any case go unrecognised and hence unanalysed. The opportunity to develop a body of law, of human rights law, which could be applied in any case of proposed sterilisation is spurned. Each case is said to turn on its own facts. As we shall see, not only is this nonsense as an argument, but it also condemns us to perpetual uncertainty in this most sensitive and highly charged area of medical practice.

The progress of *Re B* through the courts was not auspicious. As a matter of legal analysis the view was taken that the court would not have jurisdiction to enter any consent to treatment in wardship proceedings if the woman was an adult (i.e. 18 or older). At the time of the hearing at first instance she was four months short of her eighteenth birthday. The decision to opt for sterilisation had been taken some time earlier but Sunderland Borough Council, in whose care she had been since she was four, decided that it was proper to apply to make her a ward of court and then seek leave for her to undergo the sterilisation operation. Although the application was made almost a year before her eighteenth birthday, by the time the case came before the court there was a sense of urgency which pervaded the judicial proceedings: an atmosphere somewhat uncongenial, it could be said, to considered reflection on such a significant step. For, it must be remembered, what was under consideration was whether a young woman who was physically healthy, apart from being epileptic and prone to outbursts of aggression, should be sterilised out of a fear that she might become pregnant at some time in the future.

A second criticism of the way the case was dealt with was that it had reached the Court of Appeal before the landmark decision of the Supreme Court of Canada in *Re Eve*[17] was brought to the court's attention. This was a serious omission. The court at first instance, for example, may have rejected the view taken in *Re Eve* but at least it would have had to take account of it. In this way an agenda for analysing and deciding the case of *Re B* may have been set which would have forced the court to consider questions of human rights from the outset.

'Experts' and the 'Dossier'

A further, more subtle, but critically important criticism arises out of this. The court from first instance to House of Lords dealt with B's case on the basis of information compiled by 'experts' beforehand. Largely this was medical evidence. It consisted of descriptions of the girl's mental and physical condition. She was said, for example, to have a mental age of five to six years. Conclusions were expressed as to her inability to understand the link between sexual intercourse and pregnancy (although it was said that she understood the link between pregnancy and a baby), her capacity to cope with childbirth ('the process of delivery would be likely to be traumatic'!) and her lack of 'maternal feelings'.[18] It contained recommendations as to the most appropriate course of action to be taken. The whole of this 'dossier' was, in short, prepared by reference to those factors which the 'experts' thought were important. They had their agenda which they responded to and which reflected itself in the material before the court. Thus, by the time the case reached the courts, all the evidence pointed in one direction. It would have been hard for the court, even if it had so desired, to do other than follow what the 'experts' advised since their advice was based on the evidence they had compiled and the court only had that before it.

The preparation of the 'dossier', therefore, takes on the greatest significance. My point is simple. The 'dossier' constitutes the evidence on which the court decides. If it is prepared by doctors and social workers it will address matters which they regard as important or significant. They may not be the matters which a human rights lawyer would be concerned with. But, in the absence of such a lawyer being present during the compilation of the dossier and able to challenge views and ask appropriate questions, there is no guarantee that consideration of the girl's human rights will be placed before the courts. The courts will be presented with a *fait accompli*. Those who wish to challenge it will have what amounts to a near impossible task. They will have to persuade the court to reject, wholly or in part, the evidence of the 'experts', evidence that is often unanimous and which has all the trappings of expertise. It will be too late to argue that the answers may be wrong because the questions were wrong.

In my view, the court should have recognised this, should have recognised that considerations of human rights were raised by the case. As a consequence, the court should have tested the evidence for itself and, in reaching its decision, should have set down the sort of issues which doctors and other experts must address in any subsequent case in which sterilisation was proposed as an option. Sadly, the court did neither.

Instead, the approach adopted throughout and given the seal of approval by the House of Lords was to treat the case as if it merely raised a question of family law involving a child. As such, it could be dealt with routinely. The principle, that the court was to be guided by consideration of the best interests of the child, was duly incanted. Larger concerns and issues could be ignored.

Best interests

To decide any case by reference to the formula of the best interests of the child must be suspect. To decide *Re B* this way is profoundly to be regretted. The best interests formula may be beloved of family lawyers but a moment's reflection will indicate that although it is said to be a test, indeed *the* legal test for deciding matters relating to children, it is not really a test at all. Instead, it is a somewhat crude conclusion of social policy. It allows lawyers and courts to persuade themselves and others that theirs is a principled approach to law. Meanwhile, they engage in what to others is clearly a form of *'ad hocery'*. The best interests approach of family law allows the courts to atomise the law, to claim that each case depends on its own facts. The court can then respond intuitively to each case while seeking to legitimate its conclusion by asserting that it is derived from the general principle contained in the best interests formula. In fact, of course, there is no general principle other than the empty rhetoric of best interests; or rather, there is some principle (or principles) but the court is not telling. Obviously, the court must be following *some* principles, otherwise a toss of a coin could decide cases. But these principles, which serve as pointers to what amounts to the best interests, are not articulated by the court. Only the conclusion is set out. The opportunity for reasoned analysis and scrutiny is lost.

This critical view of the best interests approach brings two further points into focus. It is crucial to understand both. Together they serve as further evidence of the inadequacy of the current state of the law as represented by adopting a narrow family law approach. First, if best interests is recited without analysis, the very purpose for involving the law is defeated. If the law is to serve any purpose it must be to hold accountable those who propose to carry out medical interventions without consent, to require of them that they render an account to others. This is not because they are not trusted. Rather, it is because what is at stake is sufficiently important for the law to be involved and the law's concern is to examine the reasons and justifications for doing that which ordinarily would not be permissible in the absence of specific statutory authorisation. The best interests approach, however, is not a *reasoned* justification. If any reasoning has taken place, it has occurred prior to arriving at the conclusion that a particular course of conduct is in a person's best interests. If, as is the case, this prior process of evaluation and analysis, and the factors underlying it, go unstated, accountability cannot exist. In effect, the law abdicates its responsibility. Decisions cannot readily be challenged. Discretion becomes virtually unfettered. The disequilibrium of power between patient and doctor (and others) goes uncorrected. In the case of sterilisation, the law fails the woman-about-to-be-sterilised.

Secondly, if best interests is recited without analysis, without any recognition of the need for reasoned justification by reference to established criteria, everything inevitably is made to turn on the facts on which the judgment of best interests is to be made. This is where what I have called the 'dossier' reenters the argument. What is in truth a complex moral and social question is transformed through the device of the best interests approach into a question of fact. Is it, on the facts of this particular case, in the girl's best interests to sterilise her? And what are the facts? They are the information contained in what I have called the 'dossier'. They are the mixture of fact and opinion compiled by the 'experts'. But, you will recall that these have been compiled without reference to any check-list of *legal requirements*. They are solely matters deemed relevant by doctors, social workers and others. Thus, best interests becomes nothing other than the views of the 'experts'. Again, the law fails the woman-about-to-be-sterilised. What should be a question of evaluation, a normative issue of prescription, becomes a matter of fact, a descriptive issue.

2. Re F

Let me now turn to *Re F*. Obviously, given the criticisms I have made of *Re B*, the question to ask is whether the House of Lords did any better the second time around. The case was more complex than *Re B*. Non-consensual sterilisation again fell to be considered. But F was a mentally handicapped woman of 36. Thus, in addition, the court had to resolve a prior question: under what circumstances, if any, is it lawful to carry out medical treatment on an *adult* who is incapable of consenting. This is clearly a question of the greatest importance to the human rights lawyer. It is also a question which challenges the human rights lawyer to examine carefully what a commitment to human rights entails. The starting point for analysis will, as ever, be a concern to protect the vulnerable from real or potential oppression or exploitation. In our case, as in most, this will translate as the need to justify any proposed medical intervention by reference to carefully articulated criteria. But, the analysis must not stop at this. Oppression or exploitation may take other forms. It must be recognised that it is equally oppressive to deny an incompetent person treatment which otherwise would be judged appropriate. Whatever criteria are developed to protect the incompetent must, therefore, bear in mind that the cause of human rights is not served by so concentrating on protection of the incompetent that it is forgotten that a significant means of protecting him may be to treat him. One consequence of the failure to recognise this, or of striking the wrong balance, has been the allegation that when a patient is cared for by a human rights lawyer he may well die with his rights on!

How did the House of Lords respond in *Re F*? The first point to notice is that, as their Lordships made clear, the law was remarkably under-developed.[19] It might be thought that an issue of such importance would have long since been settled by the courts. In fact, there was no direct legal authority to guide them, proof of the fact that it is only very recently that law has been evoked as a means of regulating the relationship between doctors and their incompetent patients. (This may, of course, suggest that all was well before and the need for formal legal intervention was, and perhaps remains, unnecessary. I would argue, however, that it shows that those concerned for human rights were slow, far too slow, in establishing and clarifying the rights of the incompetent patient.)

In an effort to put an end to this uncertainty, the House of Lords made a number of significant decisions. The first was that no one in law has authority to consent to treatment on behalf of an adult, albeit an incompetent adult.

The authority of parents and guardians extends only to the care of minors. Once a child reaches the age of 16, or 18 if incompetent, parental authority and, as a consequence, the capacity to consent to treatment otherwise in the best interests of the child ceases. It may be common practice to consult and defer to parents, spouses and relatives but they have no legal authority. What then of the *court's* power as a last resort to act as *parens patriae*, to assert parental authority as the ultimate guardian of the interests of the vulnerable? This power, the House of Lords decided, does not extend to adults. It is limited to minors, expressed through the principle of wardship. Historically, wardship had been merely an example of the exercise of the power of *parens patriae*. But, the House of Lords decided, this ancient power is as a consequence of legislation now limited to minors. The larger power to make decisions on behalf of *all* who need the aid of the court, adults as well as minors, no longer exists. This led the House of Lords to the conclusion that in law even the court has no power to authorise, to consent to, any proposed medical intervention on an incompetent adult.[20]

To stop at that point, of course, would have left the law even more obscure and thrown medical practice into confusion. It would have left unanswered the question whether, in the absence of any person or institution with authority in law to consent, it was ever lawful to treat an incompetent adult. It would, as a consequence, have gravely endangered the interests of such patients if it meant that those caring for them felt uncertain as to whether they could lawfully treat them. Admittedly, some situations could easily be dealt with. Emergencies have long been recognised as justifying treatment without consent, since it is undoubtedly in the public interest to come to the aid of the person needing medical treatment in an emergency. But, short of extending the meaning of emergency so far that it could serve to justify any medical treatment, and thereby substitute a rule allowing all interventions for one allowing none, the doctrine of emergency cannot provide the answer.

This is not to say, however, that the underlying rationale of the doctrine, the public interest, cannot help us. This is what their Lordships settled on. It cannot be unlawful, it was said, to treat the adult incompetent who needs treatment, even in the absence of an emergency. If it were, the toothache of a mentally handicapped patient must go untreated. This would violate the rights of the patient and cannot be the law. Thus, the House of Lords held, the law must be that treatment is lawful if it is justified on the basis of the principle of necessity[21] or as being in the public interest.[22] And, treatment is necessary or in the public interest when it is in the patient's best interests.[23]

So far, so good. The adult incompetent will not go without treatment. But there still remains the crucial question. Under what circumstances will any particular treatment be judged to be in a patient's best interests? This is the central concern for the human rights lawyer. Make it too easy to treat the patient and the danger of abuse re-emerges. Make it too difficult and you deny the patient the right enjoyed by the competent: access to medical treatment.

Bolam

What test does the House of Lords in fact come up with to determine when it is in a patient's best interests to treat regardless of consent? The first impression is depressing for the human rights lawyer. Their Lordships seem at first sight to have settled on a most curious rule. The question whether it is in an incompetent patient's best interests to be treated is, it appears, to be analysed and answered by reference to the *Bolam*[24] decision. How extraordinary, you may say. *Bolam* is the leading case in negligence which stipulates the standard of care which a doctor must meet to satisfy his duty to his patient. It establishes that a doctor will not be judged to be in breach of his duty if, on the evidence of peers, he has behaved as a reasonable doctor. *Bolam*, in other words, is a test of competence. What, you may wonder, does it have to do with a judgment whether a proposed medical intervention is in a patient's best interests? Equally, you may wonder whether, if it is relevant to such an inquiry, it means that the House of Lords has decided to reduce to a question of professional opinion by doctors the profound question of the permissibility of non-consensual interventions. If this were indeed what the House of Lords had done it would be a dark day for medical law. In particular, it would represent a severe set back in the attempt to build medical law on a framework of human rights law. The House of Lords, it would be said, had handed over the preservation and protection of the rights of the incompetent adult to the medical profession. If a doctor could show that a number of his peers would have reached a similar view to his, this would be enough to make his assessment of what was in a patient's best interests valid and lawful. Here, if ever there was one, would be an example of the courts' craven acceptance of medical paternalism and their anxiety to slough off hard cases. Here again would be an example of the common law's unease when confronted with the language of rights.

Well, this is how the House of Lords' decision appears at first blush.[25] And, translated into the context of non-consensual sterilisation, its impact is even more troubling for the human rights lawyer. If the law were that treatment is in a patient's best interests when a doctor says it is, the House of Lords would be saying that as regards sterilisation it is permissible in law to sterilise an incompetent adult when a doctor says so, provided other doctors would agree. We only have to state such a startling proposition to realise that it cannot be the law. The House of Lords may make the occasional odd decision but they could never do anything quite this perverse!

And neither did they. In my view, their Lordships' decision, while being far from ideal, is by no means as harmful to human rights as first impressions might suggest. A careful reading of the speeches of Lords Brandon, Goff and Griffiths suggests that although the starting point was *Bolam*, the analysis is far more subtle than a mere reliance on that case. The House of Lords clearly recognised the significance of their decision and were at pains to show it. How they did so was to attach a series of conditions to the doctor's exercise of clinical judgment concerning his patient's best interests. In effect the House of Lords established that while the decision to treat without consent was for a doctor to make in accordance with the view of his peers, in making it he must give his mind to certain questions of a general nature. In other words, any doctor must, if he wishes to be judged to have behaved reasonably, give his mind to certain matters. Reasonableness then becomes, as it should be, a prescriptive rather than a descriptive term. And the prescription remains with the court, in that the court can find that failure to take account of one thing or another is unreasonable. Being unreasonable, such a failure would attract liability, arguably in trespass (battery). These matters which the doctor must consider, these questions of a general nature, are undoubtedly relatively simple in the case of a straightforward medical procedure. In the case of a procedure as controversial as non-consensual sterilisation, the questions to be asked and answered satisfactorily are many and complex.

Factors to be considered

So what are the factors which the House of Lords require the doctor to take account of? I say the House of Lords rather than any particular member of the court, since it is important to notice that what I present here is an amalgam of the views of several of their Lordships. In doing so, it could be said that I overstate the concern for human rights which I claim was shown by the House of Lords: in short, the whole which I construct is more than the sum of the parts. My response is that their Lordships were all concerned to make a central point, that the law must play a significant role in regulating a doctor's decision. That they did it in differing ways is inevitable. All I do is to bring the various strands together to make a composite picture.

Procedure

First, we should notice a preliminary point. Although not specifically a factor to be taken account of by a doctor in reaching his decision, it has great consequence as representing a clear signal by the House of Lords of its concern to act as guardian of the interests of the incompetent. The House of Lords was, as I have said, unanimous in deciding that, in the absence of a power of *parens patriae* or statutory authority, the courts in England and Wales have no jurisdiction to approve (give consent to) or disapprove of the carrying out of any medical treatment involving the touching of an incompetent adult. But, they went on, a court does have the power to issue a declaration as to the lawfulness of any procedure if asked so to do. In the case of a procedure leading to the sterilisation of an incompetent adult, because of the special circumstances surrounding such an operation, the House of Lords took the view that it was most desirable in practice to seek the court's view. Lord Bridge, expressed himself as follows: '. . . the court's jurisdiction *should be invoked* whenever such an operation is proposed to be performed'.[26]

The House of Lords then went on to stipulate the directions which are to be followed in any application for a declaration:

1. Applications for a declaration that a proposed operation on or medical treatment for a patient can lawfully be carried out despite the inability of such a patient to consent thereto should be by way of originating summons issuing out of the Family Division of the High Court.
2. The applicant should normally be those responsible for the care of the patient or those intending to carry out the proposed operation or other treatment, if it is declared to be lawful.
3. The patient must always be a party and should normally be a respondent. In cases in which the patient is a respondent the patient's guardian *ad litem* should normally be the Official Solicitor. In any cases in which the Official Solicitor is not either the next friend or the guardian *ad litem* of the patient or an applicant he shall be a respondent.
4. With a view to protecting the patient's privacy, but subject always to the judge's discretion, the hearing will be in chambers, but the decision and the reasons for that decision will be given in open court.[27]

Finally, the House of Lords then set out the form a declaration should take if the proposed treatment were judged lawful:

(a) It is declared that the operation of sterilisation proposed to be performed on the plaintiff being in the existing circumstances in her best interests can lawfully be performed on her despite her inability to consent to it.
(b) It is ordered that in the event of a material change in the existing circumstances occurring before the said operation has been performed any party shall have liberty to apply for such further or other declaration or order as may be just.[28]

These directions demonstrate, in my view, the House of Lords' commitment to human rights. As a result, the courts may not have the formal power to regulate operations for sterilisation but Health Authorities or doctors act at their peril if they do not seek a declaration. Thus, the House of Lords provides for a formal hearing. Secondly, the House of Lords requires that the patient's interests are always independently represented, usually through the Official Solicitor. Thirdly, the patient's right to privacy is protected.

Factors again
As I have said, once a case is before the court, there are certain factors which

the court will need to be satisfied of before it is determined that a proposed operation for sterilisation is in an adult incompetent woman's interests. In my view, when due account is taken of all their Lordships' views, they amount to the following:

1. That her doctors in reaching the view that the sterilisation operation should be carried out are acting in accordance with a respectable body of medical opinion skilled in the care of mentally disabled adult women.
2. That the existing circumstances of the woman which give rise to the need for the operation will continue until and unless the operation is performed and no other less serious intervention is appropriate so as to safeguard her best interests.
3. That her doctors have consulted, where relevant, specialist colleagues.
4. That her doctors have consulted members of the team caring for the woman and relatives and relevant others.
5. That her doctors have taken all due account of such factors as,
   (a) the right of a woman to control her own reproduction and not be sterilised involuntarily without the best of reasons,
   (b) the fact that sterilisation involves irreparable interference with a woman's reproductive organs,
   (c) the fact that the woman's reproductive organs are functioning normally and that the woman is healthy,
   (d) the fact that sterilisation may never be performed as a matter of convenience or to meet the needs of others, or for other improper reasons,
   (e) the fact that sterilisation gives rise to moral and emotional considerations to which many give significance and is an operation concerning which there is disagreement as to its justification among doctors and other experts,
   (f) the fact that the decision to sterilise a woman in such circumstances is a grave decision with considerable social implication.

All of these factors have, I would argue, similar weight, such that a court would need to be satisfied as regards all of them. One to which I draw particular attention is the second, that the existing circumstances of the woman which give rise to the need for the operation will continue unless the operation is performed and no other less serious action is available. Great care should be taken here. Take, for example, the facts in *Re F*. It was alleged that a male patient (P) had formed a relationship with F, a woman of 36 described as suffering from serious mental disability with the general mental capacity of a child of four to five years. The relationship, Lord Brandon stated, 'is of a sexual nature and probably involves sexual intercourse or something close to it, about twice a month. The relationship is entirely voluntary on F's part and it is likely that she obtains pleasure from it'.[29] As it happens, it appears that P had a similar relationship with other patients.[30] In such circumstances, what is striking is that it appears to be assumed that if the relationship between P and F were to continue, it was

F against whom preventive measures against her becoming pregnant should be taken. Nowhere is the question raised whether it should not be P rather than F who should be sterilised, or as regards whom some other procedure be adopted to regulate his conduct and thereby reduce the risk of pregnancy to F. Appeals were made to F's right to society, including her right to form a sexual relationship (Lord Brandon's 'it is likely that she obtains pleasure from it').[31] Such appeals are, of course, at least suspect. They can, as arguably they did in this case, serve to justify sterilising F, in the name of protecting and preserving her human rights. They can thereby serve to entrench a male-orientated approach to the management of the institutionalised mentally handicapped.[32] And, of course, those who have recourse to them seem not to be embarrassed by their lack of internal logic: F is entitled to enjoy her rights to society including sexual intercourse (and, as a consequence, should be sterilised) but she is incapable of understanding sexual relationships and their consequences (hence she should be sterilised).

The 'dossier' again

Let me now turn to what I see as the principal significance of the House of Lords' insistence on the need to satisfy certain criteria. You will remember that earlier I referred to the 'dossier' and how the information contained in it, the views of the 'experts', necessarily conditioned subsequent decisions about the best interests of the woman involved. You will remember that my criticism was that if the 'dossier' was prepared on the basis of what doctors and other carers deemed relevant, there was a real danger that the human rights of the woman would not properly be protected. By stipulating the factors to be taken account of, the House of Lords, in essence, has established as a matter of law what it is that those caring for an incompetent woman must give their minds to when considering sterilisation as an option.

The House of Lords has set out the questions which those caring for the woman must ask themselves. The views of 'experts', therefore, though relevant and important are not determinative of the question whether or not to sterilise.[33] In this way, the House of Lords has ensured that considerations of human rights, as expressed in the factors they enumerate, are of central and critical significance.

Official Solicitor's Note

Support for this view was provided by the publication shortly after the House of Lords' decision of what went under the heading of 'Practice Note (Official Solicitor: Sterilisation)'.[34] Such a Note, despite its attempt to clothe itself in the formal trappings of a Practice Direction, does not, of course, have any formal legal standing.[35] None the less, as an expression of view of the Official Solicitor and an indication of the steps which parties proposing the sterilisation of a woman must take and the factors concerning which they should provide evidence, if they are to gain the co-operation of the Official Solicitor in proceedings before the court, it is likely to be of enormous significance. And, of course, to that extent it represents a significant public commitment to respect for human rights.

In paragraph 1 of his Note, the Official Solicitor rehearses the House of Lords' view that 'the sterilisation of a minor or a mentally incompetent adult (the patient) will in virtually all cases require the prior sanction of a High Court judge'. The Note then stipulates, in paragraph 5, that 'prior to the substantive hearing of the application there will, in every case, be a summons for directions which will be heard by a High Court judge' and goes on, in paragraph 6, to say that 'the purpose of the proceedings is to establish whether or not the proposed sterilisation is in the best interests of the Patient. The judge will require to be satisfied that those proposing sterilisation are seeking it in good faith and that their paramount concern is for the best interests of the Patient rather than their own or the public's convenience'. The role of the Official Solicitor is made clear in paragraph 7: '[T]he Official Solicitor acts as an independent and disinterested guardian representing the interests of the Patient. He will carry out his own investigations, call his own witnesses and take whatever other steps appear to him to be necessary in order to ensure that all relevant matters are thoroughly aired before the judge, including cross-examining the expert and other witnesses called in support of the proposed operation and presenting all reasonable arguments against sterilisation. The Official Solicitor will require to meet and interview the Patient in private in all cases where he or she is able to express any views (however limited) about the legal proceedings, the prospect of sterilisation, parenthood, other means of contraception or other relevant matters.'

Paragraph 8 of his Note is crucial. It states that:

Without in any way attempting either to define or to limit the factors which may require to be taken into account in any particular case the Official Solicitor anticipates that the judge will normally require evidence clearly establishing:

1. That (a) the Patient is incapable of making his or her own decision about sterilisation and (b) the Patient is unlikely to develop sufficiently to make an informed judgment about sterilisation in the foreseeable future. . . .

2. That the condition which it is sought to avoid will in fact occur, e.g., in the case of a contraceptive sterilisation, that there is a need for contraception because (a) the Patient is physically capable of procreation and (b) that the Patient is likely to engage in sexual activity, at the present or in the near future, under circumstances where there is a real danger as opposed to mere chance that pregnancy is likely to result.

3. That the Patient will experience substantial trauma or psychological damage if the condition which it is sought to avoid should arise, e.g., in the case of a contraceptive sterilisation that (a) the Patient (if a woman) is likely if she becomes pregnant or gives birth to experience substantial trauma or psychological damage greater than that resulting from the sterilisation itself and (b) the Patient is permanently incapable of caring for a child even with reasonable

assistance, e.g., from a future spouse in a case where the Patient has or may have the capacity to marry.

4. That there is no practicable less intrusive means of solving the anticipated problem than immediate sterilisation, in other words (a) sterilisation is advisable at the time of the application rather than in the future, (b) the proposed method of sterilisation entails the least invasion of the Patient's body, (c) sterilisation will not itself cause physical or psychological damage greater than the intended beneficial effects, (d) the current state of scientific and medical knowledge does not suggest either (i) that a reversible sterilisation procedure or other less drastic solutions to the problem sought to be avoided, e.g., some other contraceptive method, will shortly be available or (ii) that science is on the threshold of an advance in the treatment of the Patient's disability and (e) in the case of a contraceptive sterilisation all less drastic contraceptive methods, including supervision, education and training have proved unworkable or inapplicable.'

These factors are not too dissimilar from those which I set out earlier as my own understanding of *Re F*. Both are derived from and seek to apply in a practical form certain general precepts of human rights found, for example, in the European Convention on Human Rights. Sadly, no mention was made of the Convention either in *Re B* or in *Re F*. You may think this an extraordinary omission. Had the Convention been properly considered, it would have been realised that at least three Articles, 2, 3 and 8[36] were particularly germane to the issues before the court. Whether the House of Lords' decision, as interpreted, represents a proper understanding and application of the Convention is, of course, another question to which I shall turn shortly.

There is, however, a further point to be made about the analysis I have offered of *Re F* which echoes a concern I raised earlier in relation to *Re B*. You will recall that I argued that one of the major weaknesses of the approach adopted in *Re B*, the *ad hoc*, atomising, family law approach, was that it failed to provide any adequate mechanism for holding doctors and others accountable for their decisions and actions. 'Experts' could argue that on the particular facts they formed a view in good faith and that, as a matter of law, would be that. Crucially, by identifying questions which must, as a matter of law, be asked and factors which must be considered, the House of Lords re-established a formal system of accountability, and not just any system of accountability but accountability by law in public to the courts. The significance of this cannot be overstated in terms of human rights. Recourse to discretion is confined and controlled. The rule of law, reflecting the concerns of human rights, is interposed between the incompetent woman and those who would sterilise her.

3. A counter-view

So far, in my effort to demonstrate that medical law is in truth an aspect of human rights law, I have particularly concentrated on two cases involving sterilisation. My point has been that on any analysis the non-consensual sterilisation of incompetent women raises the most profound issues of human rights. My enquiry has been concerned with the extent to which these issues are reflected in the approach of the English courts. I have suggested that while the decision in *Re B* leaves much to be desired,[37] *Re F*, although not overtly speaking the language of human rights, gets at least an honourable mention. It would, perhaps, be wrong to conclude this consideration of sterilisation, if it really is a paradigm example of human rights in medical law, without asking the ultimate question. The House of Lords took the view that non-consensual sterilisation is lawful subject to certain conditions being satisfied. Is this a valid and correct conclusion, if the question is approached from the perspective of human rights on the basis of first principles?

Let me begin, perversely, with my conclusion. It is that non-consensual sterilisation of an incompetent woman can in my view only be justified if carried out for legitimate therapeutic reasons. Conversely, it is an *unjustifiable violation of human rights if carried out for non-therapeutic reasons and, as a consequence, should be declared unlawful*. To this extent I align myself with the now famous decision of the Canadian Supreme Court in *Re Eve*.[38] Consequently, I regret the decision of the House of Lords in *Re F*, while recognising, of course, the considerable care taken in that case to come to terms with the claims of human rights. I would further argue that Articles 2, 3 and 8[39] of the European Convention on Human Rights could each plausibly compel the view I take, if properly understood and applied.

You will notice that I draw a crucial distinction between therapeutic and non-therapeutic sterilisation. This was the distinction relied upon by La Forest J. in *Re Eve*. Therapeutic sterilisation, the Canadian Supreme Court held, is permissible in law. Non-therapeutic sterilisation is not. The distinction, however, found no favour with the House of Lords. Lord Hailsham in *Re B* stated, 'I find the distinction [La Forest J.] purports to draw between "therapeutic" and "non-therapeutic" purposes of this operation . . . totally meaningless, and, if meaningful, quite irrelevant to the correct application of the welfare principle.[40] According to Lord Bridge in *Re B*, to say that [the court] can only [authorise sterilisation] if the operation is "therapeutic" as opposed to "non-therapeutic" is to divert attention from the true issue, which is, whether the operation is in the ward's best interest, and remove it to an area of arid semantic debate as to where the line is to be drawn. . . .'[41]

Lord Oliver delivered himself of the following: 'If . . . the expression "non-therapeutic" was intended to exclude measures taken for the necessary protection from future harm of the person . . . then I respectfully dissent from it for it seems to me to contradict what is the sole and paramount criterion for the exercise of the jurisdiction [*semble* wardship], viz. the welfare and benefit of the ward. . . . This case . . . involves no general principle of public policy [*sic*]. It is about what is in the best interests of this unfortunate young woman and how best she can be given the protection which is *essential* to her future well-being. . . .'[42]

Finally, in *Re F* Lord Griffiths put forward the following view: 'In Canada the Supreme Court has taken an *even more extreme* stance and declared that sterilisation is unlawful unless performed for therapeutic reasons, which I understand to be as a life-saving measure or for the prevention of the spread of disease [*sic*].'[43]

With the greatest respect, these views are hard to sustain and bordering on the perverse. The distinction between therapeutic and non-therapeutic is well known to medicine, medical law and medical ethics. Take, for example, research on human subjects, where a different regime of rules regulates therapeutic and non-therapeutic research. Of course, there are problems at the edges, but when is there not when language is employed? Had the House of Lords approached the question with an open mind, they would have realised that the key determinant in distinguishing between the two is a concept they are entirely familiar with and use every day, the concept of intention. An intervention is therapeutic if treatment (therapy) is intended thereby. It is non-therapeutic when there is no such intention. And, of course, to qualify as treatment, there must be a present intention to benefit the health of the patient. It must be a patient's *health* which is to be benefited. The benefit usually will take the form of remedying or alleviating an existing condition. Less commonly, but important for our purposes, it may (as in the case of a vaccine) protect a healthy person against an event in the future. But it is important to notice here that the difference between a vaccine against a future event and sterilisation is that, in the case of a vaccine, the event is a very real risk and the invasion is relatively insignificant. In the case of sterilisation, the latter is not so and the former may not be. Thus, any benefit in the case of sterilisation will be that much harder to show.

Let me now set out the argument. The question at its most general, and without yet taking any view about the distinction between therapeutic and non-therapeutic sterilisation, is, to what extent does the law permit the violation of a healthy person's (woman's) body without her consent to protect her from a possible future health-threatening event? Arguing from first principles, the first analytical step is to accept that some formal institutional mechanism for answering this question and thereby responding to individual cases is required. Decisions of such gravity cannot be left to private arrangement without the formal involvement of society through some institution. Secondly, such a mechanism must indicate who it is who decides whether or not to sterilise and the criteria governing such a decision. In a sense the latter is a function of the former. If doctors make the decision, then the criteria will be medical and the issue will in essence have been handed over to the medical profession. Thus, I will assert that the criteria must be established by law. This is another way of saying that non-consensual sterilisation is too important to be left to any particular group of 'experts'. The ground rules must be set by society and must take the form of law. Law is the appropriate mechanism, both so as to convey the importance of the issue and also to indicate that no social mechanism other than law is adequate to the task.

If the law should set the criteria governing non-consensual sterilisation, how is the law to do it? There are at least three approaches. The first could be that of family law through the criterion of best interests. We have seen, however, that this approach is bankrupt. It leaves us only with *ad hoc* conclusions rather than an analytical starting point for considering particular cases. A second option could be for the law to rely on what is called substituted judgment. By this a court seeks, in any particular context, to make the decision which, but for her incompetence, the woman would have made. It is founded, however, on the premise that the woman had views on the issue, which she had expressed, but is no longer able to do so because of intervening incompetence. But the cases which concern us involve women who, because of mental handicap, have never been competent. It would be a transparent fiction, therefore, to resort to an approach which claims to be giving effect to their views; they never had any. It would, in truth, merely be a device whereby others could purport to respect the incompetent woman's right to self-determination based on her alleged (but non-existent) wishes, while all the time reaching a decision which *they* want to reach.[44]

A third approach is that of human rights; that in considering the criteria governing non-consensual sterilisation, the law should begin from the position that every person has certain rights which it is the job of the law to preserve and protect. These include, with particular reference to sterilisation, the right to be free from inhuman treatment, the right to privacy, the right to life in the sense of the enjoyment of life unimpaired by the unwarranted intervention of others, and the right to reproduce, as Heilbron J. put it in *Re D*,[45] or, as Lord Brandon stated it, 'the right to bear children'.[46]

With these rights as the starting point, it would follow, in my view, that, prima facie, to sterilise someone without her consent, and consequently to threaten to violate one or more of these rights, would be unlawful. I stress the words prima facie so as to allow for the fact that there may well be circumstances in which it *is* permissible to carry out sterilisation operations without consent, but that a clear justification must be established in each case, the onus being upon the person proposing the procedure.

What valid justification could be offered? In my view, the doctor or other carer would have to satisfy the following criteria:

(a) That, given the general question posed earlier, there must be evidence that the alleged future health-threatening event would in fact threaten the woman's health. Health would, of course, need to be understood in its widest sense. This would mean, for example, that if a mentally handicapped woman was becoming suicidal because of menstruation and delusions as to what it represented, non-consensual sterilisation may be an appropriate option.[47]

It is as well, however, to notice here certain other circumstances which are advanced as health risks to the woman so as to justify sterilisation but which are much more problematical. La Forest J. identifies and responds to them in typically lucid and compassionate fashion.

The justifications advanced are the ones commonly proposed in support of non-therapeutic sterilisation. . . . Many are demonstrably weak. The [Canadian Law Reform] Commission dismisses the argument about the trauma of birth by observing, 'For this argument to be held valid would require that it could be demonstrated that the stress of delivery was greater in the case of mentally handicapped persons than it is for others. Considering the generally known wide range of post-partum response would likely render this a difficult case to prove.'

The argument relating to fitness as a parent involves many value-loaded questions. Studies conclude that mentally incompetent parents show as much fondness and concern for their children as other people. . . . Many, it is true, may have difficulty in coping, particularly with the financial burdens involved. But this issue does not relate to the benefit of the incompetent; it is a social problem, and one, moreover, that is not limited to incompetents. Above all it is not an issue that comes within the limited powers of the courts . . . to do what is necessary for the benefit of persons who are unable to care for themselves. Indeed, there are human rights considerations that should make a court extremely hesitant about attempting to solve a social problem like this by this means. . . .

As far as the hygienic problems are concerned, the following view of the Law Reform Commission is obviously sound: 'if a person requires a great deal of assistance in managing their own menstruation, they are also likely to require assistance with urinary and faecal control, problems which are much more troublesome in terms of personal hygiene'.[48]

(b) There must be a *real* possibility of the health-threatening event occurring. Furthermore, the reality of the risk must be assessed on the basis of a critically important assumption. It must be assumed that the mentally handicapped woman will already be receiving all the care and support to which she is entitled, including all appropriate steps to safeguard and protect her, given her vulnerability and susceptibility to exploitation.

(c) The principle of proportionality should apply such that: (i) there must be no less invasive means available to achieve the desired result, and (ii) the harm done must be proportionate to the risk of harm avoided. And, when considering the harm done, harm must be recognised as referring to and including physical, mental, spiritual and symbolic harm, in that the law must consider what non-consensual sterilisation may represent to the woman, to us, and as a precedent for the future.

These criteria could, undoubtedly, serve to justify non-consensual sterilisation, the aim and intention of which was therapeutic, to respond to the real health needs of the woman. Can they justify non-consensual sterilisation which is non-therapeutic? In my view, the key lies in the notion of *harm*. If harm is to be defined as I have suggested, there are certain harms, I would submit, which may not be inflicted on a person without that person's consent. The impermissibility of doing some harm, regardless of alleged benefits, without consent is recognised already in medical law in, e.g. the prohibition on psychosurgery on a mentally disordered person without that person's consent in the Mental Health Act 1983.[49]

Does non-consensual, non-therapeutic sterilisation fall into this category of harms, impermissible without consent? In my view, it does, because on the principle of proportionality, the harm avoided will never be as great as the harm done. In reaching this view, I rely ultimately on the spiritual and symbolic nature of the harm done, not merely on the physical (without for a moment ignoring this). I insist that there are things which we may not do to each other without consent, regardless of apparent (or, perhaps, real) short-term benefit. For me, non-consensual non-therapeutic sterilisation involves the destruction of an essential feature of a person's identity, of that which at a very basic level represents a sense of self. A woman may be mentally handicapped. She may have a mental age of four or five years. But if she is 25 she has many of the qualities of a 25-year-old. In particular, she has 25 years of experience[50] and has seen how women and men are treated and how they react and behave. Some sense that women are different and that the difference lies in the fact that they are women will have been acquired, rudimentary as it may be. Womanness is inextricably identified with reproductive capacity, although this may not be its only feature. To destroy irrevocably this reproductive capacity is, on this analysis, to destroy a fundamental, perhaps the only remaining, element of a sense of self. Institutionalised and ignored, the woman is now to be sterilised.

La Forest J. pointed out in *Re Eve*:

There is considerable evidence that non-consensual sterilisation has a significant negative psychological impact on the mentally handicapped. . . . The [Canadian Law Reform] Commission has this to say at p. 50: 'It has been found that, like anyone else, the mentally handicapped have individually varying reactions to sterilisation. Sex and parenthood hold the same significance for them as for other people and their misconceptions and misunderstandings are also similar. Rosen maintains that the removal of an individual's procreative powers is a matter of major importance and that no amount of *reforming zeal* can remove the significance of sterilisation and its effect on the individual psyche. In a study by Sabagh and Edgerton, it was found that sterilised mentally retarded persons tend to perceive sterilisation as a symbol of *reduced* or *degraded* status. Their attempts to *pass for normal* were hindered by negative self-perceptions and resulted in withdrawal and isolation rather than striving to conform.'[51]

In my view, this harm – in part factual, in part symbolic – is something which a civilised community should simply not contemplate. To those who say that this denies the woman the human right to society, including sexual intercourse, I respond, as I said earlier, that there is a good deal of humbug in this view. I would prefer to argue that my approach *further* protects the woman who otherwise might be the object of the sexual gratification of others who may think or be led to think that now it is safe to have intercourse with her since she has been sterilised. I conclude therefore, with the Supreme Court of Canada, that non-therapeutic non-consensual sterilisation cannot be justified in law, on the ground that it violates fundamental human rights.[52] That such a view is discomforting to doctors, carers and relatives and would make the care of the mentally handicapped more difficult may well be true. These considerations no doubt weighed with the House of Lords. But when utility and pragmatism collide with human rights it is the former which must give way. If it is otherwise, the game is lost.[53]

Conclusion

I have tried in this chapter to persuade you of two things: that medical law is an aspect of human rights law and that within medical law there is no better proof of this than the issue of non-consensual sterilisation. I hope I have convinced you of this, even if you choose to reject the particular conclusions I have reached.

Notes and references

1. See, e.g., Paul Sieghart (1989) *AIDS and Human Rights*, British Medical Association, pp. 9–11.
2. For the text of these, see Jay Katz (1972) *Experimentation with Human Beings*, Russell Sage Foundation, pp. 305–6, 312–13.
3. *Griswold* v. *Connecticut*, 381 US 479 (1965). As is well known, the Supreme Court did not hold that the 9th Amendment, *per se*, created a right to privacy, but such a right was a 'penumbral' effect of the Amendment.
4. *Roe* v. *Wade*, 410 US 113 (1973).
5. See E. Picard (1984) *Legal Liability of Doctors and Hospitals in Canada*, 2nd ed., Carswell, pp. 28, 49, 139 and generally.
6. See, e.g., *Paton* v. *United Kingdom* (1980) 3 EHRR 408, and L. Gostin, 'Human rights in mental health', in M. Roth and R. Bluglass (1985) *Psychiatry, Human Rights and the Law*, pp. 148–55.
7. Gostin, *supra* n. 6.
8. [1985] 1 All ER 643.
9. For an extensive and critical examination of the case, see Ian Kennedy (1988) *Treat Me Right*, Ch. 9.
10. See, especially, Lord Diplock, *Sidaway* (*supra* n. 8) 657.
11. [1987] 2 All ER 888.
12. *Bolam* v. *Friern Hospital Management Committee* [1957] 2 All ER 118.
13. *Ibid.*, 122.
14. *Re B (a minor) (Wardship: sterilisation)* [1987] 2 All ER 206.

15. *Re F (Mental Patient: sterilisation)* [1989] 2 WLR 1025 (CA) 1063 (H.L.).
16. See, e.g., M. Freeman (1988) 'Sterilising the mentally handicapped' in Freeman (ed.),
    Medicine Ethics and the Law, pp. 55–84; M. Jones (1989) 'Justifying medical treatment
    without consent', 5 *Professional Negligence* 178; M. Brazier (1990) 'Sterilisation: down
    the slippery slope', 6 *Professional Negligence* 25.
17. (1986) 31 DLR (4th) 1.
18. *Per* Lord Oliver, *Re B* (*supra* n. 14). 216, 217.
19. 'The argument of counsel revealed the startling fact that there is no English authority
    on the question whether as a matter of common law (and if so in what circumstances)
    medical treatment can lawfully be given to a person who is disabled by mental incapacity
    from consenting to it', per Lord Goff, *Re F* (*supra* n. 15) 1082.
20. The conclusions expressed in this paragraph are argued *in extenso* in the speeches
    of their Lordships, but encapsulated in the conclusion of Lord Bridge, that 'no court
    now has jurisdiction either by statute or derived from the Crown as *parens patriae*
    to give or withhold consent to . . . an operation in the case of an adult as it would
    in wardship proceedings in the case of a minor', *ibid.*, 1063. For the tangled legislative
    background, see the analysis of Lord Brandon, *ibid.*, 1069.
21. *Per* Lords Brandon and Goff.
22. *Per* Lord Griffiths.
23. All their Lordships were agreed on this.
24. *Supra* n. 12.
25. See, in particular, the speech of Lord Brandon.
26. *Re F* (*supra* n. 15) 1063 (my emphasis). Lord Griffiths was in the minority in urging
    that the House of Lords should change the common law so that permission of the
    court *had to be* obtained. '[O]n grounds of public interest', he stated, 'an operation
    to sterilise a woman incapable of giving consent either on grounds of age or mental
    capacity is unlawful if performed without the consent of the High Court', *ibid.*, 1081.
27. *Per* Lord Brandon, *ibid.*, 1075–6.
28. *Per* Lord Brandon, *ibid.*, 1076. You will notice the reference to the fact that any order
    took account only of existing circumstances, which could change in the light, e.g.
    of further evidence or some medical development. This was stressed by Lord Brandon
    and is of some significance, as I suggest later (*infra*, pp. 95–6).
29. *Ibid.*, 1065.
30. Private communication.
31. And see Lord Oliver in *Re B*: 'this case . . . is about . . . how best she can be given
    the protection which is essential to her future well-being *so that she may lead as full
    a life as her intellectual capacity allows*, *Re B*, (*supra*) n. 15, 219 (my emphasis).
    Previously, Lord Oliver had stated that she 'is unaware of sexual intercourse' and
    that 'it was essential in her interests that effective contraceptive measures be taken'
    because of the 'difficulty of maintaining effective supervision', *ibid.*, 216, 217. I leave
    it to you to decide whether Lord Oliver's views are compatible with each other.
32. It was Lord Bridge in *Re B* who remarked that 'the right answer is by a *simple operation*
    for occlusion of the fallopian tubes' (my emphasis), *Re B*, (*supra* n. 14) 214.
33. 'In all proceedings where expert opinions are expressed, those opinions are lis-
    tened to with great respect; but, in the end, the validity of the opinion has to be
    weighed and judged by the court. . . . For a court automatically to accept an expert
    opinion . . . would be a denial of the function of the court', *per* Lord Goff, *Re F*
    (*supra* n. 15) 1090.

34. *New Law Journal*, 13 October 1989, p. 1380.
35. See the subsequent case of *Re C*, *Times*, 13 February 1990, in which it was stated that the Note had no specific legal status and was at best advisory.
36. Article 2 provides, 'Everyone's right to life shall be protected by law.' Article 3 provides, 'No-one shall be subjected to torture or to inhuman or degrading treatment or punishment.' Article 8 provides, 'Everyone has the right to respect for his private and family life, his home and his correspondence.'
37. Not least that the House of Lords allowed only one day for the whole of the hearing!
38. *Supra* n. 17. But see the subsequent rejection of the Supreme Court's approach by the Alberta Institute of Law Research and Reform in its report *Competence and Human Reproduction*, Report No 52 (1989) which proposes legislation on the issue. *Sed quaere* the impact of the Charter of Rights and Freedoms?
39. See *supra* n. 35.
40. *Re B (supra* n. 14) 213.
41. *Ibid.*, 214.
42. *Ibid.*, 219 (my emphasis).
43. *Re F (supra* n. 15) 1079 (my emphasis).
44. See the exposure of the fiction by La Forest J. in *Re Eve (supra* n. 17) 435.
45. *Re D (a minor)*, [1976] 1 All ER 326, 332.
46. *Re F (supra* n. 15) 1068.
47. La Forest J. in *Re Eve* referred specifically to such an example, arising in the case of *Re K and Public Trustee* (1985), 19 DLR (4th) 255 (*supra* n. 17) 418–9. At the same time, however, it is as well to bear in mind what the Law Reform Commission of Canada had to say about sterilisation as a form of medical treatment. 'Sterilisation as a medical procedure', their report said, 'is distinct, because except in rare cases, if the operation is not performed, the *physical* health of the person involved is not in danger, necessity or emergency not normally being factors in the decision to undertake the procedure.' Law Reform Commission of Canada, *Sterilisation*. Working Paper 24 (1979), p. 3.
48. *Re Eve (supra* n. 15) 430–1.
49. s. 57.
50. See the excellent treatment of this point in D. Carson (1989) 'The sexuality of people with learning difficulties', 6 *Journal of Social Welfare Law*, 367–71.
51. *Re Eve (supra* n. 15) 429.
52. 'The grave intrusion on a person's rights and the certain physical damage that ensues from non-therapeutic sterilisation without consent, when compared to the highly questionable advantages that can result from it, have persuaded me that it can *never* safely be determined that such a procedure is for the benefit of that person' (La Forest J., *ibid.*, 431 (my emphasis)). La Forest J. goes on to suggest that if it is ever to be lawful, it would require action by the legislature. Any legislation, however, would, in my view, violate human rights.
53. See the critical comments of Margaret Brazier on two cases on non-consensual sterilisation decided since *Re B*, both of which are disturbing. They are *Re M (a minor) (wardship: sterilisation)* [1988] 2 FLR 997 and *Re P (a minor) (wardship: sterilisation)* [1989] 1 FLR 182. It is to be hoped that future courts would take account of Brazier's well-argued strictures and the arguments advanced in this paper. See Brazier, (*supra* n. 16).

10

Legal and political arguments for a United Kingdom Bill of Rights

ROBERT BLACKBURN

The proposal for a United Kingdom Bill of Rights may now be regarded as a central issue in legal and political debate. When first the proposal was put in a Private Member's Bill in 1947,[1] shortly after World War II and even before the Council of Europe was born and had issued the European Convention on Human Rights, it was generally regarded as an eccentric idea and wholly unnecessary. During the 1960s, in which the British government allowed its citizens to make individual petition to the European Commission and Court for alleged human rights violations, civil rights became an important political issue, strongly influenced by developments in the United States of America, especially with respect to sexual and racial discrimination and freedom of expression by the young. Lord Scarman then in 1974, in his now famous lectures *English Law - The New Dimension*, signalled the readiness of many lawyers, intellectuals and politicians to embrace a systematic code of rights to protect better a British citizen's fundamental rights and freedoms.

In the period since, the proposal has steadily gathered momentum and acceptance throughout the legal profession and across party political lines. In a recent public opinion poll 71 per cent of persons questioned believed a Bill of Rights would increase their confidence in British democracy and two-thirds supported incorporating the terms of the European Convention on Human Rights into domestic law.[2] In the form of Private Members' Bills, the proposal has passed the second chamber now in all its stages upon no less than three separate occasions, in 1979, 1981 and 1985. In 1987 a similar Bill in the House of Commons was supported by 94 votes to 16 in its second reading debate but lapsed for lack of sufficient time in which to be considered.[3] It may well be that the case for a Bill of Rights has now virtually been won, and that it is only a matter of time before a future government adopts the principle and brings forward generally accepted legislation of its own.

What are the details of the proposal as envisaged at present? The human rights principles to be contained in the document are to be similar to those

This chapter was submitted in 1989.

in the European Convention on Human Rights. Simply adopting the Convention has great advantages in that it has the added moral force of an internationally agreed interpretation of what such rights are. The Bill of Rights would give these principles the force of law in the United Kingdom, and impose a new civil obligation upon all persons, including the Crown and public officials, not to do any act which infringes any of those fundamental rights and freedoms. That obligation would be owed not simply to citizens of the United Kingdom but any person within its jurisdiction. These human rights would thus become actionable in the courts for the first time, broadening the scope of some analogous rights which exist at present such as the right not to be discriminated against under the Sex Discrimination Act 1975 or Race Relations Act 1976, and introducing some entirely new principles such as a general right of privacy.

Individual grievances

It is a strange anomaly that successive British governments and opponents of a Bill of Rights none the less support the operation of the European Commission and Court of Human Rights. Indeed the Council of Europe's work in this respect is almost universally praised. If the principle of judicial control of British law and practice is accepted from a foreign or cosmopolitan tribunal in Strasbourg, what is so different about the principle of judicial control by United Kingdom judges in London?

From the viewpoint of the citizen there would be considerable advantages in presenting one's complaint to the High Court at home rather than the present system for proceeding to Europe. But first, what cases have been brought before the court for alleged human rights violations? Over the past ten years, the Strasbourg Court has dealt with 19 cases concerning the United Kingdom, some particulars of which are shown in Table 10.1.[4]

The expense and time involved in bringing such cases are very great indeed. They far exceed anything proceedings brought before a British court would involve. In a normal case legal costs will not be less than £70,000 and only £700 is available to the petitioner in legal aid. The normal length of time taken by the European machinery is from four to six years. In addition, the Convention requires a citizen, before presenting a petition to the Commission, to have exhausted all possible domestic legal remedies. If applicable this may involve a tribunal hearing at best, or at worst an application for judicial review in the High Court with appeals up to the House of Lords in which the judiciary will inquire into the alleged injustice without reference to any United Kingdom code of basic civil rights and freedoms. Access to the Convention's scheme of human rights protection for individual British subjects therefore is at a practical level almost impossible for an ordinary

Table 10.1

Date	Name of case	Subject	Outcome
13.viii.81	Young, James and Webster	Closed shop	Breach of Article 11.
22.x.81	Dudgeon	Homosexuality: Northern Ireland	Breach of Article 8.
5.xi.81	X	Mental patient: right to have detention reviewed	No breach of Article 5(1). Breach of Article 5(4).
25.ii.82	Campbell and Cosans	Corporal punishment in state schools: respect for parents' philosophical convictions	No breach of Article 3. Breach of Article 2 of Protocol No. 1.
25.iii.83	Silver	Prisoner's correspondence	Breach of Articles 6(1), 8 & 13.
25.vi.84	Campbell and Fell	Prison visitors; conduct of disciplinary proceedings	Breach of Article 6 in two respects and of Articles 8 & 13. No breach of Article 6 on other points at issue.
2.viii.84	Malone	Telephone tapping	Breach of Article 8.
28.v.85	Ashingdane	Detention of mental patient	No breach of Article 5(1), 5(4) or 6.
28.v.85	Abdulaziz, Cabales and Balkandali	Immigration: Discrimination on grounds of sex	Breach of Articles 13. & 14 in one respect. No other breach of Article 13 or 14. No breach of Article 3 or 8.
21.ii.86	James	Leasehold reform	No breach of Article 1 of Protocol No. 1, or of Articles 6(1) & 13.
8.vii.86	Lithgow	Aircraft and shipbuilding nationalisation	No breach of Article 1 of Protocol No. 1, or of Article 14, 6(1) or 13.
17.x.86	Rees	Transsexual	No breach of Article 8 or 12.
26.x.86	AGOSI	Forfeiture by customs	No breach of Article 1 of Protocol No. 1.
24.xi.86	Gillow	Residence qualification: Guernsey	Breach of Article 8 in one respect. No breach of Article 8 in other respects, or of Article 6 or 14.
2.iii.87	Weeks	Parole	No breach of Article 5(1). Breach of Article 5(4).
2.iii.87	Monnell and Morris	Criminal appeals	No breach of Articles 5(1), 6(1), 6(3)(c) or 14.
8.vii.87	O	Child care	Breach of Article 6(1). No breach of Article 8.
8.vii.87	H, W, B, R	Child care	Breach of Articles 6(1) and 8.
27.iv.88	Boyle and Rice	Prisoner's correspondence and visits	No breach of Article 13. Breach of Article 8 in respect of one letter.

person, unless some interested lobby group association financially and morally backs his or her cause on a matter of principle. Furthermore, with such a lapse of time occurring before the Human Rights Court establishes whether or not certain conduct was wrong, it is more than likely that the practice or interference complained of has already ceased. In *Golder* v. *United Kingdom*[5] the man who complained that he was wrongly prevented from consulting a lawyer while in prison had been discharged long before the Court at Strasbourg held this to be a human rights violation. It is a moot point whether in such circumstances concerning costs, delay and remoteness, the European Human Rights Court serves as a genuine device at present for the remedy of individual grievances at all. In practice it is more in the business of giving a moral victory of principle on the inadequacy of British law.

In substance then the Strasbourg Court acts as an international verdict on British human rights standards, despite the probable fact that most past cases concerning the United Kingdom would have been decided similarly if put to a court of British judges asked to construe a Bill of Rights of the same wording as the Convention. It seems strange that it was the United Kingdom that drafted the wording of the European Convention in 1950, and also the many Bills of Rights in constitutions of Commonwealth countries, yet will not accept the self-same principles into its own law. At present we prefer what has been widely regarded as the regular national humiliation of being held to be in violation of international human rights standards in twice as many cases as any other country in Europe.

Judicial independence

One source of reluctance to incorporate the European Convention into domestic law in the United Kingdom revolves around the degree to which it would politicise the judiciary. Speaking against Sir Edward Gardiner's Human Rights Bill in its second reading debate in the Commons on 6 February 1987, Sir Patrick Mayhew, the present Attorney-General (then Solicitor-General) put this point as follows:

The judiciary must be seen to be impartial. More especially, as far as practicable it must be kept free from political controversy. We must take great care not to propel judges into the political arena. However, that is what we would do if we asked them to take policy decisions of a nature that we ought properly to take ourselves and which under our present constitution we do take. We would increase that danger if we required or permitted them to alter or even reverse decisions taken by Parliament. For a long time I have felt that herein lies the key to the general issue that we are debating. Above all, it is the factor that shapes the Government's attitude to the Bill and which leads me to be unable . . . to commend the Bill to the House.[6]

(As has been said, the Bill was supported by a large majority of 94 ayes to 16 noes on a closure motion).

Certainly an important purpose of all Bills of Rights is to promote a division of political power, so that an independent judiciary rather than government is responsible for protecting the civil rights of citizens and minorities which governments themselves are most likely to infringe. In this sense virtually all other democracies in the Western world, including the USA and most recently in the Commonwealth Canada, have 'politicised' judiciaries which are perceived as bulwarks of liberty against the state. Furthermore even if any sensible distinction can be drawn between non-political and political law, which is highly doubtful, it cannot be argued that judges at present are not familiar with dealing with litigation of a highly political nature. The Law Lords, sitting in the Judicial Committee of the Privy Council, still act as the final court of appeal in disputes concerning the written constitutions and civil rights declarations of independent Commonwealth countries and have similarly done so throughout this century in the British Empire and Dominions. The High Court today hears a huge volume of judicial review proceedings, many of which, such as the Tameside or GLC fares cases,[7] are of a far more obviously political nature than disputes concerning discrimination or privacy.

The more potent source of doubt about a Bill of Rights, especially for many members of the Labour Party, is the suspicion that British judges tend to promote establishment, conservative-minded values in their rulings. In other words, it is believed by some that the judges cannot be trusted to act impartially in balancing the conflicting general principles contained in a Bill of Rights. Professor J. A. G. Griffith has given much force to this doubt in his book *The Politics of the Judiciary*.[8] A large measure of the lack of trust is derived from the history of the trade union movement, inseparable from the Labour Party, especially at the turn of the century with the great legal set-backs it suffered in such cases as *Lyons* v. *Wilkins* (1899) and *Taff Vale* (1901), which have gone down in Party folklore. Mr Michael Foot once said that 'if the freedoms of the people of this country – and especially the rights of trade unionists – had been left to the good sense and fairmindedness of judges, we would have precious few freedoms in this country'.[9] On the other hand, one can readily think that Professor Griffith and Michael Foot might say something similar about the Conservative Party. Perhaps even for them the judiciary may prove a better protector of individual freedoms and minority rights than a Conservative majority in the legislature. And too, a Conservative under a Labour administration may prefer to trust his or her freedoms to the judiciary rather than a Labour dominated House of Commons.[10] The better question becomes whether Parliament can be trusted.

Furthermore, some critics of the judiciary have seen a Bill of Rights precisely as a device for instilling within judges a more liberal social attitude, by providing for them an express moral statement of a citizen's fundamental rights and freedoms. Thus Mr Austin Mitchell, the Labour MP, has argued:

Professor Griffith in his book on the politics of the judiciary sees the judges, rightly, as hopelessly unfit to stand between the citizen and the state. In the view of Professor Griffith and myself they are instinctively conservative, respect property, have establishment attitudes and are grovellingly servile to the executive. All that is true. We have to change that. How do we change it? We change it by educating them and by including another element in the system to which they have to pay attention. We have to introduce the rights which the [European Convention on Human Rights] will confer on the people. The judges must then listen to that and not follow their own instincts as they often do. They will have to listen to the rulings and prescriptions . of the Convention. That is an important process of education that we have to accept in our system.[11]

Among citizens generally a suspicion of establishment or social bias within the judiciary may arise from the unmistakable characteristics of its social composition. Statistics continue to confirm that collectively the judiciary is overwhelmingly male, white, in late middle-age, and drawn from a narrow social background. Research by Lord Gifford QC in 1985 showed that 4 per cent of the judiciary were women, 67 per cent were ex-public school, and the average age was 57 years.[12] *The Times* published a report in 1986 that of 800 QCs none was black or coloured, and only 19 were women.[13] Clearly the pattern of a career or proposed career at the Bar, which is a highly competitive field, appears to operate in practice to the disadvantage of women and certain social and ethnic groups; and the present recruitment of High Court judges (and the great majority of Circuit judges and Recorders) is restricted to those who rise to the top of that profession.[14]

If these doubts relating to the composition of the judiciary were tackled, a significant measure of the resistance to a United Kingdom Bill of Rights would evaporate. An official body should be set up to look into the whole system of how judges are appointed and the necessary qualifications for the work. This might be a committee of inquiry established by the Lord Chancellor, but preferably a Royal Commission (which could also inquire into the suggestion for a Ministry of Justice[15]) composed of members being politically independent or drawn from across the political spectrum. An exhaustive study and conclusions should be made on two possible ways forward. The first is to open up all judicial appointments to the solicitors' profession. This now attracts the cream of university graduates in no less numbers than the Bar, with 55,000 members compared to the Bar's 5,000, and contains a far broader social composition than among practising barristers. Under the scrutiny of a judicial appointments committee to advise the Lord Chancellor, as recommended in a Justice Report in 1972,[16] solicitors might be made eligible to hold any judicial office for which they possessed the necessary experience and aptitude for the post. With solicitors gaining rights of audience in all courts, and being of equal competence in legal research, the numbers of such appointments would be likely steadily to rise. The other option to be considered is for a career judiciary. A career judiciary, as practised elsewhere in Europe, would make an immediate impact upon the social homogeneity of our judges, with trained professionals taking responsibility in their thirties, women not being prejudiced in their career by taking periods off to start a family, and with an active policy of equal opportunities.

The present government in its recent White Paper on legal services,[17] and the Opposition parties in their 1987 election manifestos, all envisage important changes in our legal institutions which should affect the composition of the judiciary. By encouraging this process and achieving some generally acceptable reform of the judicial appointments system and a consequent widening of the social composition of the judiciary, there will be a greater public confidence in the administration of justice generally. This would greatly facilitate political acceptance of a United Kingdom Bill of Rights.

Arguments about entrenchment

An essential aspect of Bills of Rights is that they control future legislative enactments. In other words they give power to the judiciary, or the special court set up to apply the document, to invalidate any provisions in later statutes or subordinate legislation which in the opinion of the judges is contrary to the principles expressed in the Bill of Rights. To institute such an arrangement in the United Kingdom poses interesting problems going to the heart of its jurisprudence.

The traditional view of such a proposition, the entrenchment of a corpus of fundamental law superior in status to ordinary parliamentary Acts, is that it is impossible. This is because the first principle of the whole British legal system is the doctrine of parliamentary sovereignty, whose three traits Professor A. V. Dicey laid down to be,

first, the power of the legislature to alter any law, fundamental or otherwise, as freely and in the same manner as other laws; secondly, the absence of any distinction between constitutional and other laws; thirdly, the non-existence of any judicial or other authority having the right to nullify an Act of Parliament, or to treat it as void or unconstitutional.[18]

When the House of Lords set up a Select Committee to report on whether a Bill of Rights was desirable in 1977, it accepted that there was no way in which a Bill of Rights could be made immune altogether from amendment or repeal by a subsequent Act. Their specialist adviser drew on judicial precedents such as *Vauxhall Estates* v. *Liverpool Corporation* (1932) and *Re Ellen Street* (1934)[19] to evince a conclusion that clauses in a Bill of Rights purporting to apply to future legislation would be inoperable and a conflicting later statute would always prevail, even if the contradiction was merely implicit. Thus all offensive statutes passed after a Bill of Rights would be upheld. The Bill of Rights as a statement of law at all would be progressively eroded.

Politically such legal arguments when applied to a Bill of Rights do not make sense. All constitutions are in essence political. They are born of political purpose, they describe political facts, and they depend upon political acceptance. If Parliament convenes a new political arrangement, it is very unlikely the judges will refuse to accept it. The question is not what the judges *can* do, but what they *will* do. If they accept the purpose of the Bill of Rights, they will find means of judicial principle to follow. If the measure were railroaded through Commons and Lords in the teeth of opposition, it might prove difficult for judges wholly to accept its purpose. However, if the measure had a clear consensus of all-party support, and perhaps the moral backing of a referendum in its favour as well, judges would not assert a superior political right to reject it founded upon legal precedent. They would welcome its purpose. Means of facilitating acceptance in legal doctrine might include two particular devices. Firstly, as H. W. R. Wade has suggested,[20] the terms of the judicial oath of office might be altered by general agreement to include a reference to the Bill of Rights. Secondly, the Lord Chancellor might submit a Practice Statement for approval by the House of Lords referring to the special position of the Bill of Rights, in the same way that in 1966 the House of Lords by Practice Statement made the important change in legal doctrine that it was no longer bound by its own earlier decisions.

However, such direct confrontation with legal dogma is best side-stepped. The secret for doing so has come to be regarded by many – including Lord Scarman – as to look instead to including a clause in the Bill of Rights which successfully creates a new rule of statutory interpretation. A legislative presumption would be placed in our legal reasoning. This would be to the effect that in the construction of any provision in any statute passed after the Bill of Rights, it will be presumed that Parliament intended the provision to operate within the limits of the Bill of Rights and not to have any meaning or effect in contradiction of its principles. Such a formula was recommended by the House of Lords Select Committee in its Report in 1978[21] and has been adopted by the draft legislation presented to Parliament since. Its latest drafting, in clause 4 of the Human Rights Bill 1986, is as follows:

No provision of an Act passed after the passing of this Act shall be construed as authorising or requiring the doing of an act that infringes any of the fundamental rights and freedoms, or as conferring power to make any subordinate instrument authorising or requiring the doing of any such act, unless such a construction is unavoidable if effect is to be given to that provision and to the other provisions of the Act.

There is good reason to suppose that this device might serve to entrench the Bill of Rights in all but form. For it is by this means that the courts themselves have come to give primacy to European Community legislation over later domestic enactments. Such superiority is clearly recognised by the European Court of Justice and was the intention in the European Communities Act 1972, section 2(4) of which reads, 'any enactment passed or to be passed . . . shall be construed and have effect subject to' Community law. This has been taken to lay down a very strong rule of statutory interpretation, a presumption that Parliament in its legislation since does not intend to legislate contrary to Community law. Furthermore, it is a legislative presumption that goes beyond others which simply serve to clarify the meaning of uncertain or ambiguous words or phrases in a statute. According to Lord Denning the primacy of Community law over future enactments by Parliament will only be displaced by the statute expressly stating that it is to have effect in contradiction to Community law. He said in *Macarthys* v. *Smith*

If the time should come when our Parliament deliberately passes an Act with the intention of repudiating the Treaty or any provision in it or intentially of acting inconsistently with it and says so in express terms then I should have thought it would be the duty of our courts to follow the statute of our Parliament. I do not however envisage any such situation. . . . Unless there is such an intentional and express repudiation of the Treaty, it is our duty to give priority to the Treaty.[22]

The courts have therefore recognised the constitutional significance of the United Kingdom's partnership in Europe and found means of judicial principle to accept and enforce its purpose. It is wholly to be expected that the judiciary will similarly recognise the constitutional significance of a Bill of Rights and apply similar judicial reasoning to accept and enforce the primacy of its human rights principles over future parliamentary measures.

Modernising the constitution

The case for a Bill of Rights has two associated purposes: the remedy of individual grievances, and the limitation of political power. The latter rests upon the argument that the United Kingdom's constitution has not adapted to developments in the twentieth century, which have combined to place an excessive concentration of political power in the hands of the political party in office and especially its leaders in Cabinet. A Bill of Rights is within the spirit of the principle that 'if there is to be a free society there must be the maximum tolerable division of political power'. These are Lord Hailsham's words,[23] and his thesis that today an elective dictatorship operates within the British political system has been widely accepted but remains to be redressed. A Bill of Rights would have the effect of placing a constitutional limit upon the political power of parties in office.

What are the changes that have occurred in the twentieth century to alter the constitutional balance which previously existed? The pivotal shift has been in the social policy of government. Whereas previously government interfered very little in the ordinary lives of citizens, it has come to be expected to take responsibility for virtually all aspects of social and economic welfare, and in the process there is now hardly any part of our working or private lives which is not regulated by the state. Government has become an actively interventionist exercise.[24] The second great change has come about in the relationship between government and Parliament. Previously governments could not automatically rely upon their majority of party members in Parliament to support any piece of legislation they proposed. As remains the case in Congress in the USA, members of the legislature tended to vote according to their party colleagues in government but retained, in Walter Bagehot's words, 'a lukewarm partisanship'.[25] Since 1918 a rigid party discipline has emerged so that by virtue of the government's majority in the Commons Cabinets may legislate upon any matter at their discretion.[26] Neither has the second chamber, the House of Lords, the political power it once had to secure more than minor amendments. Lacking credibility in its unreformed composition, it now possesses no more than the authority to delay a government Bill for one year even in matters of fundamental constitutional or human rights concern.[27]

The last great change that has occurred is that today constitutional respectability is claimed for any item of government legislation – regardless of its human rights implications – upon the notion that the party in power possesses a 'mandate' from the electorate. Since universal adult voting was introduced by the Representation of the People Act in 1918, it has regularly seemed in party politics as if anything can be justified upon the simple moral basis of an electoral majority.[28] This confusion of democratic principle, 'moral populism' as it has been called,[29] poses special dangers to human rights of which J.S. Mill warned 130 years ago.

The will of the people . . . practically means the will of the most numerous or active part of the people; the majority or those who succeed in making themselves accepted as the majority. The people consequently may desire to oppress a part of their number; and precautions are as much needed against this as against any other abuse of power. The limitation, therefore, of the power of government over individuals loses none of its importance when the holders of power are regularly accountable to the community, that is, to the strongest party therein.[30]

Conclusion

A survey of High Court, Court of Appeal and House of Lords judgments in the 12 months to December 1988 reveals at least eight reported occasions upon which the bench made reference in some way to the European

Convention on Human Rights. Although technically the Convention is no part of Britain's law, it is with increasing frequency that judges do in fact refer to its human rights principles for persuasive authority, to help explain the moral issues in the case before them and how British law fits into these principles. The more often such judicial *dicta* take place the more likely it is that later judgments may discuss the Convention, for a growing body of precedents now exist for it being permissible and helpful to do so. A watershed was reached in *Attorney-General* v. *Guardian Newspaper (No. 2)* – the *Spycatcher* case – where all three Lord Justices in the Court of Appeal and three of the five Lords of Appeal in the House of Lords made reference to the Convention. Lord Justice Bingham cited with approval Lord Fraser's earlier suggestion in *Attorney-General* v. *BBC*[31] that

this House and other courts in the United Kingdom should have regard to the provisions of the Convention for the Protection of Human Rights and Fundamental Freedoms and to the decisions of the Court of Human Rights in cases, of which this is one, where our domestic law is not firmly settled.

It is time to permit British courts of justice to go further than this. The Convention's human rights principles upon which we all agree should be firmly implanted in British law through a new Bill of Rights, to equip and modernise the United Kingdom's constitution for the twenty-first century.

Notes and references

1. Preservation of the Rights of the Subject Bill.
2. Cited in the parliamentary debates on the Human Rights Bill 1986, HC Deb., Vol. 109, Col. 1227.
3. Human Rights Bill. For a survey of the Bill and its parliamentary progress, see Robert Blackburn, 'Parliamentary opinion on a new Bill of Rights', *The Political Quarterly* (1989), p. 469.
4. As at 13 July 1988. See HC Deb., Vol. 137, Cols 214–16.
5. [1975] 1 EHRR 524.
6. HC Deb., Vol. 107, Col. 1267.
7. *Secretary of State for Education* v. *Tameside M. B.* [1977] AC 1014 and *Bromley B.C.* v. *GLC* [1983] 1 AC 768 respectively.
8. (3rd edn, 1985).
9. *The Guardian*, 16 May 1977.
10. Lord Hailsham thought so when in Opposition in the 1970s: see *The Dilemma of Democracy* (1978), Ch. XXVI.
11. HC Deb., Vol. 109, Col. 1241.
12. *Where's the Justice* (1986), p. 25.
13. Cited in Rodney Brazier, *Constitutional Practice* (1988), p. 255.
14. For the existing qualifications at law, see the Supreme Court Act 1981. In 1985, 29 of the 373 Circuit judges were solicitors (Gifford, *supra* n. 12).
15. See Gavin Drewry, 'The debate about a Ministry of Justice', *Public Law* (1987), p. 502.
16. *The Judiciary* (1972).

17. *Legal Services: a framework for the future*, Cmd 740.
18. *The Law of the Constitution* (9th edn, 1939), p. 91.
19. [1932] 1 KB 733 and [1934] 1 KB 590 respectively.
20. *Constitutional Fundamentals* (1980), p. 37.
21. HL [1977–8] 176.
22. [1981] 1 All ER 111 at 120.
23. *The Dilemma of Democracy* (1978), p. 95.
24. See J.M. Keynes, *The End of Laissez-Faire* (1926).
25. *The English Constitution* (1867; Fontana edn, 1963), p. 159. Bagehot warned that 'if it were otherwise, parliamentary government would become the worst of governments – a sectarian government'.
26. For early criticisms of this development, see M. Ostrogorski, *Democracy and the Organisation of Political Parties* (1902), and R. Muir, *How Britain is Governed* (1930), Ch. IV.
27. See S.A. de Smith and Rodney Brazier, *Constitutional and Administrative Law* (6th edn, 1989), Ch. 16.
28. Generally see A. H. Birch, *Representative and Responsible Government* (1964).
29. H.L.A. Hart, *Law, Liberty and Morality* (1963), p. 77.
30. *On Liberty* (1859; Pelican edn, 1974), p. 62.
31. [1988] 3 All ER 545 and [1980] 3 All ER 161 at 176 respectively.

11

The European Social Charter

PAUL O'HIGGINS

The European Social Charter is one of the least known of the instruments laying down international labour standards.[1] It is one of the oddities of life that it appears never to have been referred to in any judicial proceedings in courts in the United Kingdom, as a recent scrutiny of the Lexis database seems to indicate.[2] Many MPs seem unaware of its existence and both the CBI and the TUC pay relatively little attention to it, although they are now giving it more regard than they did in the past. For these organisations, for the TUC and the CBI and for other workers' and employers' organisations, other labour standard-setting bodies, such as the European Community and the International Labour Organisation, loom much larger in their consciousness. None the less, the European Social Charter is an important instrument which embodies certain important principles. It is very largely influenced by the International Labour Organisation, which participated in the drafting of the Charter and also in certain stages of the scrutiny stage of the investigation of compliance with the standard laid down by the Social Charter. The Charter is almost unique in that contracting states do not have to accept all the obligations contained therein. Of course, as an international lawyer, one would expect to find in many treaties reservations, but in principle reservations would appear not to be compatible with the European Social Charter. A number of states have submitted reservations, but the view of the Council of Europe is that those reservations are not in any way compatible with the terms of the Charter, therefore they can be ignored and difficult questions can be avoided.

Accepting obligations

The Charter was drawn up under the auspices of the Council of Europe; it came into force in 1965 and the first state to ratify it was the United Kingdom. However, the first state to denounce any of its obligations under the Social Charter was *also* the United Kingdom. There is a certain ambivalence on the part of the United Kingdom in relation to instruments of this kind. About a third of the members of the Council of Europe have adhered to the Charter. A few states have accepted all its obligations, but the Charter,

---

This chapter was submitted in 1989.

as I have said, is almost unique in that it allows adhering states to opt for five out of seven principal articles. In addition to those five out of seven principal articles, they must opt for other articles or paragraphs so that they have either adhered to ten articles altogether or at least 45 paragraphs. The Charter gives states very considerable freedom to pick and choose which of the obligations they will undertake to adhere to. So it is all the more sad to report that the degree of non-compliance is rather higher than one would expect in a treaty of this kind, given that states do not have to adhere to any obligation other than those they freely choose to accept.

General principles

Part One of the Charter lays out certain general principles, essentially of social policy. In the course of the nineteenth century, for a variety of motives, some of which were exclusively humanitarian, steps were taken by more advanced European countries to seek to lay down labour standards that should be accepted by these states themselves as well as by states with which they had trading relations. One of the motivations was to ensure by law that less advanced countries should not undercut labour costs in the more advanced industrial states; and that has remained a consideration in the elaboration of international standards. Equally important are the more humanitarian and human ideas that the adherence to decent labour standards contributes to social peace, which of course in turn contributes to world peace.

So Part One of the Charter lays down a series of propositions or targets that in a sense embody a policy that has been elaborated in Western Europe since the middle of the nineteenth century, and which has been further refined in the twentieth century under the aegis of the International Labour Organisation. Just to pick a few examples: 'Everyone should have an opportunity to earn his living in an occupation freely entered upon.' That is very largely concerned with the freedom of choice of workers to enter particular occupations. 'All workers have the right to just conditions of work.' 'All workers have the right to safe and healthy working conditions.' 'All workers have the right to a fair remuneration sufficient for a decent standard of living for themselves and their families.' This last, picking at random the fourth of the targets and principles underlying the Social Charter, goes very deep historically. It is present in a paper delivered by John Kells Ingram to the British Trade Union Congress meeting in Dublin 1880.[3] You can find it also in the judgment of my cousin Henry Bournes Higgins, as President of the Australian Arbitration Court, in the *International Harvester* case in 1907; and you find it above all in the Treaty of Versailles 1919, embodying the constitution of the International Labour Organisation where this principle is spelled out in the words that 'Labour is not a commodity'.[4] That of course has a number of meanings, but the prime meaning is that the pricing of labour cannot be left exclusively to the operation of market forces, but on the contrary arrangements must be made to ensure that all workers have an adequate income to supply a reasonable standard of living for themselves and for their families.

Checking reports

Part Two contains the specific obligations which adhering states are free to accept or not as they wish; Part Three deals with the underpinning of the obligations; and Part Four deals with the supervisory system. The supervisory system essentially is scrutiny of regular reports made by contracting states as to their compliance with the terms of the Charter. These reports are scrutinised by an independent committee of experts who refer their reports to a ministerial committee consisting of one member from each of the contracting states. The ministerial committee in turn refer their comments to the Parliamentary Assembly of the Council of Europe, and at the end of the day the report, the ministerial committee's comments and the Parliamentary Assembly's comments go to the Council of Ministers of the Council of Europe, who may make recommendations.

The wording of the Charter envisages that the recommendations would be made to individual contracting members, for example saying to state X, 'Watch it – you are not in compliance with such and such an Article.' But in practice most of the Council of Ministers' recommendations have been of a very general kind. There is a certain friction between the ministerial committee and the committee of independent experts, in so far that as I may indicate to you what I believe the Charter requires where there is a difference, I take the view of the Committee of Independent Experts.

Difficult areas

What I would like to do is to single out a number of particular Articles for comment in relation to the situation in the United Kingdom and the United Kingdom's obligations. Over the years in which the Charter has been in force there have been something like ten cycles of reports of independent experts commenting upon reports submitted to them by the contracting states. The contracting states submit regular reports to the Council of Europe indicating what they are doing to comply with their obligations. These reports are sent to representative organisations of employers and unions in the country concerned, but it is very rare, particularly for a British organisation, to comment upon the British government's reports. When the Committee of Experts sits down armed with the government's report on the one hand and the Social Charter on the other, the question before the Committee is: is the government complying with the terms of the Charter? One of the difficulties is that the evidence is provided solely by the government itself, unless some body, like the Low Pay Unit in the United Kingdom, has itself volunteered gratuitously to provide evidence or the relevant social partners have provided evidence. The Committee of Experts usually have only their own expertise to draw upon and they need not necessarily have a member who is acquainted with the law and practice of the state whose report is being examined. The Committee of Experts consists of just seven members, although the contracting states adhering to the Charter number 14.

One of the areas that has given rise to difficulty for the United Kingdom is Article One, with its obligation for the United Kingdom to ensure the right of a worker to earn his living in an occupation freely entered upon. The interpretation of this obligation is that, among other things, it underpins the obligation that there should be no forced labour. It is one of the oddities of modern life that Britain has been singled out over the many cycles of the investigations by the Committee of Experts as not being fully in compliance with this obligation not to permit forced labour. The stumbling block is the Merchant Shipping Act 1970, section 89, which is a relic of the nineteenth century position whereby breach of contract by a worker was a criminal offence. Gradually, as Britain became more civilised, the idea of breach of contract being a crime was thrown out, leaving only seamen as a group of workers whose simple breach of contract could be a criminal offence. There are two forms of action that can be taken. First, a criminal fine or imprisonment can be imposed upon seamen who disobey orders or neglect their duty, and secondly, more controversially, the Act makes special provision for the extradition of deserting seamen. One thinks of extradition in terms of criminals fleeing from one country to another, but historically extradition also developed in a very different area from that of deserting seamen. So the residue of the notion that only seamen when they break their contracts commit a crime is found in the provisions of the Merchant Shipping Act 1970, section 89, which provide a summary procedure whereby a deserting seaman from a ship registered in another country may, if that country has entered into treaty obligations *vis-à-vis* the United Kingdom, be surrendered, without any adequate enquiry as to whether or not he is properly accused of deserting, to the captain of a ship from which he is alleged to have deserted.

As a result of the criticisms of the independent experts, Britain has agreed with a number of states to abrogate its treaty obligations. So Denmark, the Netherlands, Germany, Greece, Norway and Spain have all agreed with the United Kingdom to put an end to the surrender of deserting seamen. But Britain still has a number of such obligations with other states which it has not yet put an end to. Therefore the Independent Committee of Experts regularly comments unfavourably upon this fact.

Article Two defines 'just conditions of work', such as the need for a minimum two weeks' annual holiday with pay, and so on; the need in fact to ensure an adequate weekly rest period. There are no particular problems with regard to the two weeks' annual holiday with pay, which may well be enjoyed in practice in Britain. But this is neither guaranteed by law nor by collective bargaining.

Article Three sets out the right to safe and healthy working conditions. No particular problem exists there, save with regard to the obligation of the contracting state to provide for the enforcement of safety and health regulations by measures of supervision. There is a problem here that, I think, the British government has not given the highest priority to keeping the number of safety inspectors up to their full complement.

Article Four deals with the right to fair remuneration. In Paragraph One, the high contracting party undertakes to recognise the right of workers to remuneration such as will give them and their families a decent standard of living. It is a matter of great controversy how validly the Committee of Experts has interpreted this obligation of how to quantify what is a remuneration such as to give a worker and his or her family a decent standard of living. The Committee has suggested a rough and ready rule of thumb, saying that an adequate wage should be at least 68 per cent of the average national wage. This figure was arrived at after a great deal of research both by the Council of Europe and by the OECD, so it is not a figure plucked from the air. This 68 per cent of the average wage represents the 'decency threshold' below which workers in any member country should not be allowed to fall. Additionally, it is suggested that the average male manual/non-manual industrial wage, and the average female manual/non-manual wage, must be applied in each case to the appropriate category. There has been, particularly in relation to women workers in the UK, a considerable gap on occasion between the 'decency threshold' and the actual level. It was found in 1984 that 70 per cent of female manual workers fell below this decency level. This is a matter which is raised regularly by the Low Pay Unit. The British government argues that there are other factors to be taken into account, such as the various social security benefits that are available to those in receipt of low pay. There are difficult legal questions whether a social security benefit available to people receiving low pay satisfies the obligation of the Charter, which does not in fact talk about recognising the right of workers to an income such as to give them a sufficient standard of living. In other parts of the Charter there is reference to an income which can be obtained by wages or by social security benefits. Here the reference to *remuneration* is what is obtained in exchange for labour, and so it may not be an adequate response to the criticism implicit in some of the findings about the decency level that one must also take into account the social security benefits and tax benefits available to the low paid. The argument is unresolved and may possibly, at some stage, be subject to judicial scrutiny.

Article Four contains other obligations, including the right of workers to a reasonable period of notice for termination of employment. In virtually every report – and there have been ten reports of the Independent Committee of Experts – the Experts have singled out the period of notice to terminate contracts of employment in Britain, so short as to be derisory, as not being compatible with the Charter. In particular, they point out that the statutory minimum one week's notice after four weeks' service does not go up to two weeks until the expiry of two years' service.

Article Five guarantees the right to organise, and the freedom of workers to organise to protect their interests. There are unresolved difficulties here as far as the Committee of Experts is concerned and we await their next report to see how they view the 'GCHQ affair', where the government unilaterally took away the right to belong to an ordinary trade union from its employees on the grounds of its decision being in the interests of national security. Whether that is compatible or not with the Charter remains an open question and the Committee of Experts look forward to receiving full information on that in their next enquiry.

Article Six deals with the right to bargain collectively. The contracting parties undertake to promote joint consultation between workers and employers, to promote where necessary appropriate machinery for establishing negotiation between employers and employers' organisations to regulate terms and conditions of employment by means of collective agreements. This does give rise to difficulties in the UK, and I think one has to summarise the issue fairly succinctly. To what extent are reasonable working standards best obtained by allowing the labour market to operate freely, with a nudge here and a nudge there, but basically leaving it unregulated? How far should minimum standards be decided by law or by certain other procedures, thereby interfering with the free operation of the labour market? If the abolition of collective bargaining – temporarily one assumes – for teachers' pay is taken into consideration, one may feel that Britain is not perhaps complying with this obligation to promote collective bargaining in that particular area.

There is a particular difficulty with regard to the last part of Article Six, which is exceptional in international labour instruments in laying down explicitly a right to strike. It is not an unqualified right. It is a right of workers and employers, so it applies equally, allowing employers the freedom to take lock-out action in cases of conflict of interest, but not in a conflict of rights. In other words, the freedom to take collective industrial action against either side in industry is not extended to cover a dispute about the interpretation of existing contracts or existing agreements. It is about where one is arguing to create a new relationship, which means at the end of the life of a collective agreement a dispute about what the new conditions of employment should be in a dispute of interest. A dispute about the proper interpretation of the terms of the current contract of employment is conflict of right. The right to strike is limited to disputes of interest. It is limited secondly by the terms of any collective agreements that lay down a procedure for the settling of disputes. Furthermore, it is subject by Article 31 to such restrictions as are prescribed by law and as necessary in a democratic society to protect certain important recognised rights. One has a difficulty here because the terms of the Charter have been interpreted to indicate that a right to strike means at the end of the day that workers may not be penalised for having taken part in that strike. Let me repeat the point, if you have a right to strike, there is a clear distinction between when it is lawful to strike and when it is unlawful. The strike is lawful if it is within the area permitted by Article Six, paragraph four. It is unlawful if it is outside that area. The employer is then free to take what actions he thinks appropriate to deal with that particular matter. The problem is that there is not, in the sense defined in the Charter and as understood by the independent experts, a right to strike in English law. Let me give two simple examples.

The first was a case decided many years ago called *Cruikshank* v. *Hobbs*[5] where a group of stable-lads and -lasses at Newmarket took part in an official strike organised by the Transport and General Workers' Union, over terms and conditions of employment. It was an unpleasant, prolonged stoppage, at the end of which the racehorse trainers, who were the employers in this case, found that they had fewer horses to train than they would have liked, and, therefore, they made some of their employees redundant. It was not unreasonable, it might be thought, that they chose to make redundant those who had been disloyal enough to take part in the strike. They did not dismiss those who had been loyal and remained at work during the continuance of the strike. The Employment Appeal Tribunal had no difficulty in reaching the conclusion, which is sound English law, that to select people for redundancy on the basis of their past disloyalty to the employer, evidenced by their taking part in an official strike, is a perfectly legitimate ground of selectivity for redundancy. I remember at the time being in France and my French colleagues were wholly shocked by this. It was said, 'Are you savages in your country to allow the dismissal of lawful strikers?' The right to strike means that if one takes part in a lawful strike then one thing cannot happen: participation in that lawful strike cannot be used as grounds upon which to subject one to a detriment.

The second example is, of course, Wapping. Under English law it is possible for an employer lawfully to dismiss his entire workforce if they strike. Perhaps in anticipation, fearing that something like Wapping might happen, the Committee of Experts has indicated that mass dismissal of workers in the course of industrial action is not compatible with the provisions of Article

Six, paragraph four. In other words, there are difficulties if the United Kingdom is to come into line with its obligation under Article Six, paragraph four.

Article Seven, the right of children and young persons to protection, is basically concerned with young people. Here, too, an embarrassment has been headed off by British indications to the Committee of Experts that a review of the employment of children has been taking place. Of course, a review did take place some years ago and legislation was actually adopted in the light of that review, but that legislation has not yet been brought into force. What happens at the moment is that the employment of children is partly regulated by education legislation and partly regulated by byelaws. The Committee of Experts reported recently that English byelaws permit young people between the ages of 13 and 15 to work for 27 hours a week during school holidays. Young people over the age of 15 and under the age of 18 may be permitted to work during school holidays for 37 hours a week. Young people of 13 and above may be employed for an hour in the morning before going to school. It has been questioned whether that is compatible with the need for young people, and children, to enjoy adequate protection. Again Article Seven concerns the remuneration of young people, and talks about fair remuneration. The Wages Council Act of 1986 removed young people from the protection of wages councils, and so one is left with the problem of whether young people in Britain are adequately protected. There are actually two problems: whether the abolition of all minimum wage standards for all workers is compatible with the article dealing with young people and also whether it is compatible with the article providing for the need for all workers to enjoy an adequate remuneration.

Article Eight gives rise to a controversy. It deals with the right of employed women to protection. It is a moot point how far the special rules govening the employment of women are compatible with modern notions of equality of treatment of men and women, and so one could argue that there is nothing particularly illegitimate about the government's denunciation of its obligations under this Article. But it is, sadly, the first denunciation by any member state of an article of the Social Charter. At first sight, one would say that common sense dictates equal treatment for men and women. This side-steps a difficult problem. Under the auspices of the European Economic Community, much research has gone into the deleterious effects of continual night work *on male workers*. There is, therefore, an argument, which has been suggested by a number of organisations in the United Kingdom, that prolonged night work is damaging to the health of everybody, and that, therefore, there should be regulations not only on night work by women but also on night work by men – that night work itself needs, to be regulated. Remember, all that Article Eight, paragraph four says is that the member states agree to regulate the employment of women on night work. It does not regulate night work for men.

It appears that there are a great many negative attitudes in the United Kingdom revolving around the notion of social rights and international labour standards. They could be seen, sadly, in Mrs Thatcher's speech in Bruges, where she was concerned about social engineering from Brussels. It is an issue which has got to be faced fairly and squarely. Over a period of 150 years up to 1970, various general propositions of social policy about the need for a decent wage for all people at work were accepted by a large number of the more civilised countries in the world. Britain has made a major contribution in laying down standards which have been adopted in the past by the International Labour Organisation and by the Council of Europe in the European Social Charter. Many of the ideas there were ideas developed by British labour practice in the past. Paradoxically, since 1963 every improvement in labour standards within Britain has been the result of the adaption of standards from outside. The whole issue of equal pay comes from the Rome Treaty. It does not come from a very strong women's movement persuading the government to enact legislation in that particular way: it comes from outside the country. Not only do we have this period from 1963 up to the mid-1970s where labour standards were adopted because of membership of international bodies external to the United Kingdom, but since then there has been a sharp conflict of policy, two views being possible. Do we believe that the best way of ensuring the widest distribution of the good things in life, the best way of ensuring the reduction of poverty, the increase of employment, the removal of hardship, the caring of the old, and so on is best left primarily to the operation of market forces where the state plays a role as a long stop? Or do we continue to share the policy implicit in the Social Charter that it is necessary to have rules over a wide range of matters rather than leave these matters to be regulated merely by market forces. Of course, it is also possible to reject the idea of rights at all in this area – but that is a different tack altogether. It is in fact a position adopted by some people, namely that the proper business of human rights lies with civil and political rights, the right to vote, freedom of speech, freedom of assembly, freedom of association, the right to property and so on. Somehow social rights are seen as an illegitimate addition to the category of human rights.

In my opinion, social rights are an essential element in the adequate protection of human rights of all kinds and I hope that the United Kingdom does not go too far in the direction of abandoning minimum labour standards embodying the social rights and continues to recognise the importance of protecting, by international treaty and by national legislation, certain basic rights in the area of social and industrial relations.

Notes and references

1. On international labour standards in general, see Paul O'Higgins, 'International Standards and British Labour Law', in Roy Lewis (ed.), *Labour Law in Britain* (1986) at pp. 572–94, and N. Valticos, *International Labour Law* (1979).
2. See a valuable article by Noreen Burrows on the 'United Kingdom', in A.P.C.M. Jaspers and L. Betten, *25 Years: European Social Charter* (1987) at pp. 27–51, especially p. 29. The Council of Europe's Social Charter is not to be confused with the draft European Community Charter of Fundamental Social Rights currently being discussed. For the text of the latter, which is based in part upon the Council of Europe's Charter, see *Trade Union Information* (Published by the Commission of the European Communities), issue No. 3/89, at pp. 7–10.
3. John Kells Ingram, *Work and the Workman* (3rd edn, 1928), especially at p. 8.
4. Treaty of Versailles, 1919, Article 427.
5. [1977] ICR 725.

Index